Moonchild

Moonchild

The Story of an Indigo Child with Asperger's

Melanie Ockwell

A Self-Published Title
Animal Dreaming Publishing
www.AnimalDreamingPublishing.com

Moonchild

A self-published book produced with the help and support of
ANIMAL DREAMING PUBLISHING
PO Box 5203 East Lismore
NSW 2480 AUSTRALIA
Phone +61 2 6622 6147
www.AnimalDreamingPublishing.com
www.facebook.com/AnimalDreamingPublishing

First published in 2015
Copyright text © Melanie Ockwell
Copyright cover art © Melanie Ockwell

www.MoonChildBook.com

Also available as an e-book
To download go to www.MoonChildBook.com

ISBN 978-0-9923983-8-5

Designed by Animal Dreaming Publishing
Edited by WordCircus.com
Printed in Australia

Life through my eyes

This book would never have seen the light of day without the love and support of my family. My husband Mark, my rock, my hero.

My daughter Tyler, you give me strength when I have none.

My daughter Kyra, your compassion shows no bounds, I'm always in awe.

My son Ethan, your love of life inspires me.

My best friend Kim, for being The Lighthouse Lady.

My friend Suzie, for inspiring me to go further.

I am so grateful to all my family and friends for sharing this journey of life with me.

Thank you for being exactly who you are.

xx

Contents

Contents

Introduction

I believe that Asperger's Syndrome is a natural way of responding to a world changing at an increasing speed.

My reason for writing this book is to tell everyone that there is more to Asperger's Syndrome than the many defects of the diagnosis. Hidden within Asperger's Syndrome lie many gifts! Asperger's Syndrome is an Autism Spectrum Disorder, which is characterised by significant difficulties in social interaction and communication.

My hope for this book is to make people more aware of the gifts that Asperger's Syndrome can bring and how these gifts in turn can be nurtured and valued more highly in the future than they are now.

I believe that Asperger's Syndrome is a natural way of responding to a world changing at an increasing speed. Change is everywhere, and for people on the spectrum it gives little time to adjust. I feel like I'm walking on rocky ground most of the time, trying to find my feet.

The following pages are my life and my views, and it is not my assumption that all people with Asperger's feel the same way as I do, as I really do not know. It isn't my intention to upset anyone either; this is my way of seeing my diagnosis and what that means to me.

In the following pages I speak about what it means to be an Indigo child. Indigo is a term first used by Nancy Anne Tappe and many authors have written on the subject since. Indigo children are a New Age concept and these children are believed to possess special, unusual traits and abilities. I first came across the term Indigo while I was studying youth work at university. Then I read the book, *The Indigo Children* by Lee Carroll and Jan Tober, and I identified with the concepts instantly.

I finally felt that there were people out there who understood the parts of me I tended to hide from everyone. For those of you who haven't read or even heard of the concept of Indigo it speaks of an evolution of new kids being born who are extremely sensitive to their surroundings, who don't just observe life but feel it in every pore of their skin. It speaks of children so sensitive that they can immediately pick up when someone is lying to them. They are sensitive enough to pick up vibrations that others cannot perceive, such as the emotional turmoil of others, or the impressions of what is happening in the lives of the people around them that those people themselves may not even know. They are 'empaths' that absorb just about every vibration around them.

I have included all the books that are relevant to this book in the list of further readings, and I ask that before you read on, you open your mind and heart, as the concepts here are not your average run-of-the-mill. I have opened my heart and my soul in the writing of this book, and I lay it out before you all in the hope that you will treat people on the spectrum more gently and hopefully understand them more fully; and finally recognise that it's not all symptoms of a diagnosis but reactions to a world that is overwhelming and mostly unjust in its quick judgements of everyone. May people who are on the spectrum finally be recognised as the wonderful gifts that they are and already contain within them, gifts that seem to go unnoticed when being diagnosed.

Do I profess to hold all the answers? Absolutely not! Each individual on the spectrum is exactly that: an individual, and their diagnosis is only a small part of who they are. I believe parents are the key players in their children's lives and development; it's not just the psychologists, speech therapists and occupational therapists that reign supreme in unlocking the potential in these uniquely gifted children. The professionals are there to help and guide you but they are not the be all and end all. Life is like a giant jigsaw puzzle and each person in your child's life holds a piece of knowledge that your child will benefit from: uncles, aunts, cousins, friends and professionals, all working together, can help to unlock the gifts your child holds. Your job as a parent—and the hardest job of all—is to facilitate who and what information you need to best assist your child and yourself. Your task now is to do what is in the best interests of yourself and your child, whatever or wherever that may take you. I'm sharing my journey with you so that you have another perspective that you may not have encountered so far.

I have been battling my whole life to return to the person I was when I was a small child, a time before the world pressed upon me and told me that everything I was and believed was somehow wrong or flawed. I keep trying to get back to the time when I felt I was accepted, as I was free from the judgement of others. When life was simple and made more sense. When I listened to the voice deep within my soul and trusted the whispers of wisdom they would always steer me in the right direction and I was free to explore the world and all its beauty.

Sometimes I have fallen in a hole and needed the help of others to escape the depths of depression that have crashed down on me from time to time, so yes, there was bad stuff too, but the voice within always told me what to do. My mother explained it as my guardian angel; she taught me to always trust this voice and it will never steer me wrong. My mother also taught me that there was a not-so-good voice that would always get you into trouble and helped me understand that it was best not to act on this voice.

I have tried to live my life this way whenever I can. When I listen to my guardian angel and not to my ego, my life seems to flow in a series of coincidences that let me know I am on the right path. When the coincidences disappear and I start to feel depressed, I realise I have strayed from my path. This might sound crazy to some but this is what I have found works best for me. I have read about it happening to others so I know I'm not the only one. I wonder if living this way will help other Indigo/Asperger children.

I identify more with the term Indigo than with the term Asperger, though both terms help me work out who I am as a person. I couldn't have one without the other. My world wouldn't make sense.

My heart goes out to everyone who loves or knows someone on the spectrum, or is uniquely gifted and not understood, as the path is rocky, with many ups and downs. I just hope that you find more ups and fewer downs. It is during the times of turmoil in my life that I have found some of the greatest insights and learnt the most. I hope you can take some heart in that. Good luck on your path.

The Early Years,
Before Autism

With my hero Julie by my side,
I knew I would always be safe.

Before I ever knew what autism or Asperger's Syndrome was, before I had ever heard it spoken about by anyone, I always thought I was a normal, typical little girl.

The only reason I felt different was that I was born with club feet, a condition where your feet are turned inward so they clap together and don't lie flat on the floor when standing. Therapy began immediately, so that later in life I would be able to stand, walk, and—if I was lucky—run. My feet were put into special boots, which were joined together by a metal bar to help keep them flat. My specialist decided that this was the best course of action as opposed to cutting tendons and ligaments in my ankles. At 18 months of age I began to take my first steps, only I had to walk while balancing on butterfly bolts under my feet, which attached the bar and kept my feet in place. I succeeded in my steps though some family members thought the sight of my struggling steps cruel and harsh.

"Take the boots off," they said. But my mother

persisted and by the age of around two years I no longer needed the boots as my feet had become flat as I had grown.

I remember wearing the boots and I don't remember any pain or discomfort as I didn't know any different. I do remember the 'clang' the bar made when I banged it on my parents' wooden furniture. I loved the sound it made as I struck it. I also remember that my mum wasn't all that pleased with me doing this. Looking back now I know I put many scratches in the furniture, and Mum got a few dints to her knees as well.

As I got older my parents would tell me that the doctor's prognosis of my condition was that I would walk but I would never be able to run. Nearly as soon as the boots came off though I was either climbing or chasing after our cat, Tom. Climbing was fun; I had no fear at all. I would climb my wardrobe and enjoy the view from atop it. (There were no built-in robes in the 70s). I would have been about three or four at the time, but as good a climber as I was I could never get back down. This never stopped me though and I would wait until my mum would wonder where I had got to and find me sitting happily on top of the wardrobe. She was always amazed at how I had gotten so high. I felt her sense of wonder and enjoyed it, I never noticed the concern she showed.

Sometimes I even climbed on to the roof of the house. I only did it when I knew my mum was preoccupied with guests, as she used to watch me like a hawk. I would climb a tree that was just outside my bedroom window and I could easily climb on to the roof from there. I loved the way everything looked from up there, I felt as if I was on top of the world and I could see the far horizon. There was a beautiful view of a steeple in the distance, and I wondered how far away it was and if one day I would be able to find it and go inside the fascinating building. Of course my poor mum would come searching for me and yell at me when she discovered where I was. Apparently I gave my position away because they could all hear me clomping about on the roof. If only I had been a little quieter, I thought to myself, Mum would leave me here longer and I could take in the wonderful view for longer.

I spent much of my childhood alone even though I was the youngest of seven children. My brothers and sisters where much older and had left home and started families of their own. I was what my parents called 'a change of life baby'. My mother was forty-five and my father was fifty when I was conceived. They thought of me as a 'surprise'.

Almost every time I was alone in the backyard I would climb something. One of my favourite spots was on top of a woodpile my father had stacked up against the side fence. I would climb up there and call out to our lovely neighbour, Mrs Turnball. Mrs Turnball would hear or see me and come out and talk with me. She also would give me treats like biscuits and lollies, which I loved. I could never climb down so I would wait there until my mum would come and retrieve me, which she always did.

Cats were my other source of enjoyment and fun. They were my furry playmates that I could dress up and push around in my dolls' pram. Poor old Tom, he was my first and best friend. I would play in the backyard for hours with him. Looking back, I can't understand why Tom let me humiliate him by dressing him up in pink frilly dresses and matching bonnets. Maybe he knew he was my only friend. I have an old, 22 millimetre movie of me climbing the woodpile and pushing Tom around in my pram. I still think fondly of Tom as my old friend. One day I was told he had been hit by a car. Poor Tom, I thought to myself, and I expected him to be dead, but he wasn't. He had crawled under our next door neighbour's house and nothing and no one could coax him out. Apparently someone saw him drag himself under there as he was paralysed from the waist down. I missed him very much and I think he stayed under the house for about three months. Mrs Keirns, the lady on the other side to us, would leave food under her house for him.

When Tom did finally come out my mother decided

it would be a good idea to take him to the vet, but she had a lot of trouble trying to get him into the car. My brother Lance and his partner where holding him inside the car but old Tom was having none of it! He was scratching and clawing like he had gone completely mad. For a paralysed cat he was putting up one hell of a fight. Out of sheer desperation they thought that maybe he would go to the vet if I went with him and they handed Tom to me. Immediately he calmed and sat quietly in the back seat with me. All was well. Tom was sitting quietly on my lap and everyone stared at me in disbelief, as the wild cat of a few minutes ago was calm. We all thought we might just make the trip until they turned the key and the engine started to run. Tom didn't hurt me but I wasn't strong enough to hold onto him.

"Looks like Tom doesn't want to go to the vet," they said, and no one dared try to make him.

Tom continued his life for another six months or so until a dog finally caught up with him. Most of the people in our street knew the story of old Tom and how he was my best friend, so the neighbours who found Tom buried him in their backyard where they had found him to save me the grief of seeing him like that. I was extremely sad that I wasn't able to say goodbye to my best friend but I also understood why our neighbours buried him.

A couple of months later I was given a new kitten, a tabby. I expected the new kitten to be just like old Tom, so I played and cuddled him the same way I had with Tom. The new kitten, unbeknown to me at the time, hated it! I recall playing with the new kitten in a wooden row boat that Dad had in the backyard. I remember squeezing the kitten in a tight cuddle and then letting it go as it pulled away from me. The kitten couldn't get away fast enough, and scampered up a large post that divided the front yard from the backyard. The kitten sat on the top of the pole for a couple of minutes before it turned its head and looked directly at me. Then something strange happened. I heard the kitten's voice inside my head say, "I'm going now, and I'm not going to come back!"

Well I was shocked and devastated, shocked that I heard the kitten and devastated by what it said, so I went running inside to tell my mother what the cat had said to me. I can't remember my mum's response, but I'm sure she would have tried to reassure me that the kitten would come back. It never did though.

So, heartbroken once again, I had started to forget about my furry friends when a friend of the family came over one day with a unique-looking little bundle of fur. She was almost all white with a round spot of ginger on her head, a larger black spot on her left side, a small black spot under her chin and a tail that was black and ginger stripes all the way to the tip.

Mum said, "Her tail looks like it has been taken off another cat and stuck on her!"

She was right, it did look a little odd. When it was time to name this strange little bundle of fur I decided to name her Julie.

"Are you sure you want to call it that, Melanie? It's a person's name."

"Yes I'm certain, Mum. My new best friend's name will be Julie."

Julie and I quickly became almost inseparable and she allowed me to play with her the way that Tom used to play; dress-ups and into the dolls' pusher she went. She would let me wheel her around the backyard almost all day and at the end of the day the sound of her purr would help me to fall asleep at night. Life was perfect again, as I had a new best friend.

The following year, at age four, I started school at Gowerville Primary School in Preston. When it was time for pet parade, my best friend was even allowed to come to school with me! I was so excited. Julie hated all the dogs that were at the parade that day but as long as she and I were together she could put up with them. Julie won a ribbon and certificate for the pet with the longest tail and I was so proud! I loved school and some of the teachers, but Mrs Pearce was my absolute favourite. I never had many friends, only a couple that I would sit next to in class or play with at lunchtime. Most of the time I missed my friend Julie.

One day after school I was playing in the front yard when a man with a big Alsatian came walking up the street towards our house. I was terrified because I knew this man used his dog to intimidate and frighten people, and they were coming straight for me! I didn't know what to do. I was scared and glued to the spot on the footpath. My trusty friend Julie came from out of nowhere and gave that Alsatian a hiding it wouldn't ever forget, and I was relieved when it went yelping back to its owner. How did Julie know I was in trouble? I don't know, but I knew with my hero by my side I would always be safe.

Another time I was playing in the front yard again under the giant weeping willow tree when the lady's dog next door somehow got out. This lady was single and kept the dog for protection and it would savage anyone it didn't know. And guess who it came straight for? Yes, me again of course. I would have only been around five years old at the time. I quickly scrambled into my dad's boat, which he had been rebuilding, and I only got up and out of the way in the nick of time while the dog was growling and snapping at my feet as I pulled them into the boat. The dog stayed growling, barking and jumping up trying to get me. I thought I would be stuck in there for hours or until someone came outside to see what all the fuss was about. No one came, and the dog just stayed there waiting for me to get back down. I didn't know what to do! Again Julie came from nowhere to rescue me, giving that nasty greyhound a few good clouts on the end of its nose, before it too went yelping back home. With Julie there with me I again felt safe and climbed out of the boat and went inside to tell my mum what had just happened.

My mother later told me that one day while I was at school that the same dog had dug its way into our backyard and our cat Julie was waiting for him when he finally squeezed under the fence. She smacked that dog so hard and so fast that it didn't have time to get back under so it jumped clean over the six-foot fence. The greyhound never attempted to dig into our yard again and Mum was relieved.

I loved my cat so much and was so grateful to her for protecting me that I decided that I wanted to be a cat. The look of horror on my parents' faces when I started eating the cat's dry food out of her bowl put me off a little, but not enough to make me stop. She was my friend and I wanted to be just like her. My parents continued to discourage this behaviour and finally put a stop to it, but all I knew was this cat was my friend and loved me completely, more than anyone else I had met so far at school and in the neighbourhood.

All the kids seemed to want to play a game called 'doctors and nurses'. At first I thought this game was fun, one person would play the doctor, another a nurse, and someone else had to be the patient. I wanted to be the doctor so I could mend people and make them better, but I always seemed to end up being the patient. I was told this was a game that all the kids played and it was a secret game that adults and parents shouldn't be told about. At first I was sceptical but most of the kids who lived around my neighbourhood all wanted to play this game with me, so maybe they were right when they said 'all kids played this game'. It all started off so innocently, then the rules kept changing. If you were the patient you had to be naked, just like in real life, and it seem to escalate from there. I started to hate this game but I just couldn't seem to get out of it. I just wanted someone to play with and I really wanted to fit in so I did what I was told.

One night I was sitting on top of our back fence looking into a rear backyard watching a fire burn and crackle and pop. I was mesmerised by the fire, the smell of the smoke, the warmth of the flames, the different colours and smells and all the different sounds the fire made as it burned. I was so at peace sitting there that I didn't notice a man walk towards the fire.

He startled me with, "Hello there little girl, what you doing up there?"

"I'm watching the fire," I answered, hoping he would leave and go back inside his house.

"Where are your parents?"

"Inside."

He came right over to me. "You're a pretty little thing, aren't you?"

I was flattered that he thought that, but I also felt uneasy, as he was in my personal space now. I just wanted him to go away so I could continue to watch the fire. Then without any warning, he bundled me up in his arms and was holding me against him. I was scared and didn't know what to do. His breath stank like salami or something just as offensive and I pulled back a little, but a five-year-old was no match for an adult male. I was thinking about how I could I get away when I heard a sound. It took a couple of seconds for me to recognise what it was: the sound of a zipper being undone! Shit! Not him too, I thought. Isn't he too big to play this game? It was then I heard a voice my head say, "Ask him what he is doing in your most innocent voice." And I did just that.

"What are you doing?" I asked.

The man stopped for a second, seemed to wake up or realise where he was or something and, luckily, put me back on the fence. I stayed and watched the fire for a little while I guess; I was in shock at the thought of what might have happened if I hadn't listened to the voice in my head. I gave thanks to whoever it was and went inside.

Animals never wanted to play these games with me, so I fell in love with them all the more after that. Looking back now, I can see how my Asperger's had made me an easy target. I found it hard to believe that people could lie; I couldn't understand why someone would even want to. I was naïve and so eager to be a part of a group, any group, that I was somewhat unaware of the whirlwind that was circling me at the time. I was vulnerable to people who had ulterior motives. It is something that, over the years, I have sadly come to expect from some people. Every situation in which people have manipulated me has made me aware of how it has broken me; broken my soul, my sense of peace, love and excitement to be alive. The moments of my realisations are my darkest hours, during which I struggle to come back from and see the love and beauty in all things once more.

Now where was I? That's right, back to when I was five years old again. One weekend we had family over visiting and earlier that morning my father— dear old Dad as he used to call himself—had the old wooden ladder out cleaning the leaves from the gutters. I was playing in the backyard with a niece when I noticed my beloved cat Julie at the top of the ladder on the roof of our house. Oh no, I thought, I must save her! I was too young to understand that she could climb down by herself. So I slowly started to climb the ladder, with my niece just behind me, when I heard a voice inside my head say, "The ladder is going to fall, tell your niece to get down." I turned and looked down and told her that the ladder was going to fall and that she had to get off. She refused and so I told her again, more urgently, that she needed to get down. I watched as she took her last step off the ladder and reached the bottom. As soon as she had taken that last step the ladder started to fall.

I can't remember falling but I remember waking up on the ground with my body lying on the grass and my head lying on the concrete. When I started to get up I felt a sharp pain pass through my left arm but it eased as I stood up. I went inside and told my mother that I had fallen off the ladder and that my arm was still a bit sore. Mum looked me over and I seemed fine, so we all tucked into my favourite jam doughnuts for lunch. Jam doughnuts would have to be one of my favourite foods. After lunch we all went into the lounge room to watch TV. I can't recall what happened next as apparently I passed out, but was later told that my eyes rolled up until only the whites were showing and then I collapsed. Mum started screaming hysterically and my dad had to slap her to snap her out of it. I do remember waking up in the back of an ambulance only to throw up over Mum's favourite fur handbag. I apologised before passing out again. I awoke again and I was in hospital and the nurses where asking me to count to ten for them. I just wanted to sleep but I hazily complied. The whole time they kept asking me if my parents had hit me on the head with a hammer.

"No," I would slur. "I fell off the ladder."

Again and again they continued to ask me as I drifted off to sleep. I spent a week at the Royal Children's Hospital in Melbourne. I only saw my parents maybe two or three times the whole time I was there. I couldn't understand why they would just leave me there. I was scared and felt very alone. Later I found out that the hospital made my parents feel very uncomfortable as they thought that one of them had hit me on the head with a hammer. And I can forgive them for thinking that; I know they were only trying to protect me. Apparently the hard baubles on the hair ties I had been wearing when I fell onto the concrete went inside my skull and left a hole the exact shape and size that a hammer would. No wonder they were questioning me so much about how it happened.

So a little over a week later, with my head shaved on one side where they had operated and pulled the bones back to where they should be, and with stiches from my left ear to the top of my head, I went back to school wearing a baseball cap to hide how awful my head looked. Mum took a couple of pictures before I went to school but I didn't like anyone looking at my head so she only got two. The amazing thing was that when I returned to school not one child teased me even though I was ready for it. I went to school with an extreme comb-over and a cap and no one said a word. Inside, I was very grateful for that. I know my mum had a chat with the school before I returned but I have no idea what she said. Whatever it was, it worked. No one even looked sideways at me.

I felt so lucky to be alive after the fall from the ladder. Years later I found out that I was millimetres from becoming brain damaged as the bone of my skull was pushed in so far that it was almost touching my brain. In some X-rays it looked as though it was and my parents were told that it was certain I would have a brain injury of some kind. I look back now and think just how lucky I was but I also wonder about the voice I heard that day. Where did it come from? How did it know the ladder was going to fall? Why did I have to fall? To this day I am still confused. I'm not a religious person but maybe it was my guardian angel trying to warn me about what was to come? At least I saved my niece from the same fate, and maybe that's all I was meant to do.

My co-ordination was out of whack after the

accident and the school wanted to keep me down a grade but my mum wouldn't hear of it. It took time but I slowly regained all the skills I had lost before the accident. Once I was feeling better and my hair had slowly started to grow back, I started spending my afternoons with my friend from school. She lived across the road from school so I could play with her on my way home. We would roller-skate together and it was one of my favourite things to do. My best friend Julie the cat was always waiting for me when I came home and would sleep with me every night. Mum later told me that Julie didn't cope so well when I was in hospital. She wandered the house crying and meowing. She cried so much that she almost drove my parents crazy. Mum felt sorry for her and would talk to her and let her know what was happening with me when no one was around. When they shaved my head they gave Mum my hair, and Julie was so inconsolable that Mum gave her my hair. Well Julie played with that lock of hair like it was one of her kittens. She would throw it up in the air and chase it. She took it everywhere with her and she stopped crying.

Julie was my constant, my companion, my best friend. She made my childhood peaceful and happy especially in times when I was frightened and confused. Cuddling her would wash away my worries and fears. No matter what was happening around me I felt loved by her and my parents and felt safe with them, even when my life was threatened by my brother-in-law, who had threatened to kill me because my parents wouldn't tell him where my sister had escaped to. The threat only lasted a couple of weeks when my brother-in-law took his own life. I was sad for my sister and my nieces and nephews but relieved he didn't carry out his threat.

But my parents took the threat seriously and kept weapons at the front and back doors of our house. My dad made sure I would get to school and back safely, so instead of walking as I usually did, he would put me on the back of his motorbike. It was a little scary but I loved the thrill of it. It was exciting! The kids at school asked me why my grandad was picking me up from school.

"It's not my grandad," I would retort.

But it got me wondering about my own grandparents and when I'd hear them all talking about visiting their nana on the weekend I began to feel sad about not knowing my grandparents, who had died before I was born. I remember crying in bed one night wanting what all the other kids seemed to have, a relationship with their grandparents. I cried myself to sleep. It was in the middle of the night when I felt a sensation I'd never felt before. I looked up and could see the misty shape of a figure standing in my room. I knew it was a grandparent. I don't know how I knew; I just had that knowing feeling I guess.

It frightened me terribly and I put my head under the covers, shaking uncontrollably. "Please leave, thanks for coming but you're scaring me," I said. Eventually, with my head still under the covers, I must have drifted back to sleep. I awoke the next morning and told Mum what had happened. She believed me and said she had an idea of which grandparent it could be. I never cried again for not having my grandparents in my life because I knew they were still with me although they were a bit scary and I didn't want them waking me up in the middle of the night again.

I would have loved to be able to talk to someone about these things. My mum listened and believed me although it only made me feel more different as I was told not to talk about these things because people wouldn't understand.

Julie made the stressful times in my life less stressful; whenever I was with her I felt peace and didn't worry so much about everything going on around me. We shared a special connection that I can't quite describe in words as it is something that has to be felt. Like love I guess, the word means something different to everyone, and it's something you have to experience to truly understand the meaning of.

By the time I turned eight, my mum had her heart set on moving out of the home she had lived in for over thirty years. She decided it would be best to move to Lakes Entrance.

"Where the country meets the sea," she said.

She had had enough of city life and longed to return to the country where she had grown up. Country life seemed to call to her. I hated the idea! She wanted to move to a place where there were no footpaths, no electricity, no running water, and no telephone. Nothing! All I could think about was leaving my friend behind and where was I going to roller-skate with no footpaths or made roads? The packing lasted six months before we finally moved to a block of land just outside Lakes Entrance. A block of land and that was it: home. The garage was the first building to be erected, so we slept in the garage and used the smallest caravan you have ever seen as our kitchen. Our things were all packed tightly into the garage and what didn't fit was simply sitting outside on the ground. It must have looked quite a sight to anyone who drove past. We had an old outdoor toilet that Dad constructed himself with leftover material he had gathered together from somewhere. I hated the toilet as everyone kept telling me to be careful of Red-back spiders on the toilet seat. The toilet was bad enough and I had to worry about spiders as well! We heated up the camp shower in the sun all day until it was warm enough to use. I didn't mind all this, as I loved nature and thought the whole thing was exciting, except for the Red-backs. It was interesting living this way. I was a little worried about the Blue-tongue lizard living under my bed, but Mum kept telling me that it wouldn't hurt me as it was more interested in catching flies and bugs. Mum also said that where there is a Blue-tongue there are no snakes. Snakes! Bugger. I hadn't even given a thought about snakes. Yikes.

Dad called our arrival at Lakes Entrance 'The Landing', just like it must have been when the First Fleet settled in Australia. With no power and water I can understand why he said that now. My dad loved sailing ships; it was his passion.

My parents did most of the work themselves on the garage with help from my older brothers. They constructed and concreted the floor themselves and I was amazed by what they could accomplish when they all worked together. I loved exploring the new countryside I found myself in, and the ninety-seven acre farm behind us became my favourite stomping ground. I chased lizards, caught grasshoppers, and invented contraptions to catch rabbits. It was a magical time for me. My friend Julie came along though Mum didn't want to bring her to the country as she was afraid she would become feral. I begged her to let her come with us and she did. She never became feral like Mum had thought she would. She was still my best and only friend. I also fell in love with the horses that roamed the farm behind us, and when I wasn't out exploring my new surroundings by walking the hills and valleys, I was getting myself acquainted with these beautiful animals. I had always wanted a horse but living in Melbourne had killed that dream.

Starting a new school was hard as I didn't know anyone and hardly anyone wanted to be my friend. I couldn't understand why. I was nice to everyone; I never was hurtful or mean. I heard that you were not considered a local until you had lived in the area for 15 years or so and I assumed that maybe this was the reason for my failed attempts at friendships and trying to fit in. Work began on our house that my parents had designed themselves, nothing flashy, something simple that suited them. My parents did most of the work on the house themselves, more out of financial reasons than anything else. Leaving the harder work to the professionals, our house was built with a lot of love, sweat and tears and you could feel it when you entered it. I was so happy when we finally had a toilet we could flush and a room of my own to sleep in with a proper bed.

Over time I made a couple of friends, but nature and the animals were what always welcomed me when I came home. I understood them better, and they were easier to get along with; they just made more sense to me. I continued to explore the land around me and would disappear for hours. I could walk over the hills, past the sheep and the horses and sit next to the North Arm, which is an estuary that winds itself around the landscape before going back out to the sea. I would sit beside the Arm in quiet contemplation. I loved the way the sunlight danced along the top of the water. I would look about me and see large wombat holes dug deep into the earth. I was tempted to climb in one so that I could see a wombat but thought better of the idea as I had been told that wombats had large claws for digging and they tend to crush animals that come into their den as they are very strong. I came face to face with lizards, snakes, goannas and rabbits on my walks and it all was very exciting for me. I really wanted a rabbit—no I mean *really* really wanted a rabbit—and not just any rabbit; I wanted a wild rabbit. They were everywhere, wild bunnies playing and dancing on the hills as the sun was setting, their little white tails bobbing up and down in the distance. I would watch them frolic and enjoy themselves until they disappeared into their burrows. It was after a few failed attempts at trying to capture them—one being a crate with a carrot on a stick dangling on a piece of string—that I hatched a plan I was sure would work. I could dig the bunnies out! To be honest I'm not really sure exactly when I decided on the 'Dig Out Plan' but I thought it was an awesome idea, find a rabbit burrow and start to dig and then continue to dig until I found a rabbit, then I would quickly grab him and keep him for myself. I found a small warren that didn't seem to have any other exits and started to dig. I was digging for what seemed liked hours, I'm not exactly sure how long I dug for but it was a while. I never rested, I was going to keep digging all night if I had to. I wasn't going to stop until I had caught myself a fluffy little pal. I thrust the shovel into the ground again and again; finally the shovel came down on the object of my greatest desire, almost chopping the poor thing in two. Luckily I noticed just in time and I reached down and grabbed up the little bunny. As I did this the bunny let out a strange, high-pitched sound. It almost sounded as if it were screaming for its life. I recall the sound hurting my ears and making me feel terrible but I can't quite recall the actual sound the poor thing made. While it was still making the squealing sound I held the young bunny tight against my chest and ran home to show my parents that I had caught myself a rabbit, despite what they had previously thought. I was so proud of myself. My memory fails me on what happened next to the bunny; I know I named it but cannot for the life of me remember what I named it. I'm not sure how long the poor wild creature lived in captivity. It wouldn't have been very long as most wild animals do not fare very well as domestic pets. I guess that was the main lesson I learnt from catching that little bunny, that some things that are in the wild, need to stay in the wild. That part is now burnt into my memory for all time.

On my walks I found a walnut tree and would sit under it for ages cracking and eating walnuts. I would pat the horses and even ride one of them, no saddle, no helmet, no reins. I felt as free as the horses and I would let them take me where they wanted to go. I always felt safe when I was exploring, it felt like I had someone watching over me, protecting me. My parents created a lovely vegetable garden and orchard where they grew nearly all the food we ate and we had tank water to drink. My parents liked to live off the land and be as self-sufficient as possible. So whenever I was hungry I went out to our backyard and picked something. Looking back, it was the best way to eat, as I was never really hungry. It was nice to graze as the animals did, and for someone with undiagnosed Asperger's it was the best thing my mum did for me. My mind was clearer and I was happier and felt excited by every day. Living at the end of a long lane was very lonely at times as there were not many children who lived close enough to play with. The land became magical to me and I loved to show anyone who came to visit the beauty of it.

One day I met a girl who was camping in the lane on school holidays with her aunt. I took her to my favourite spot under the walnut tree. She stopped and went a little ashen and said she had seen a man in a flannel shirt standing at the top of the hill watching us. Thinking we might be in trouble from the owner I started probing her with all kinds of questions. She was a little shaken and said that he disappeared. I thought that maybe she blinked and missed him leave. So I hurried home to see if I was in trouble or not. I arrived home and no one said anything so I took my new friend home. I did find it strange that she no longer wanted to play with me any more when I went to visit her again. The aunt's excuses seemed plausible so I tried not to think about it too much, as she was going home in a few days anyway. About a year later I was playing with my best friend from school in the same area, when she looked up to the same place and said she had seen a ghost of a man wearing a flannel shirt. This time I freaked out as she repeated everything my holiday friend had told me the year before. I never saw the man myself but I always felt that someone was watching and I felt protected by it. I felt that the spirit of this man was somehow trying to keep me safe while I explored, so I continued to do so.

When I was about eleven my best friend surprised me by swimming across the North Arm with her dog. I couldn't believe she had swum that far. I knew it must have been dangerous but she said it wasn't that bad and it only took 10 or 15 minutes. Normally to visit each other we had to go into town and if you walked it could take up to two hours. I was so excited to see her unexpectedly. So this became our new way of visiting each other. My mum told me not to do it, as I wasn't a very strong swimmer and the Arm was full of weeds that she worried I would get tangled up in and drown—which would be a real possibility, but because I had already done it successfully, I couldn't understand her concerns. So my friend and I would continue to meet this way in secret.

One night I had arranged to meet my friend on my side of the Arm. I would have dry clothes and a towel waiting for her when she arrived. The scrub was thick and the hill I had to climb down to get to the edge was steep and it felt even steeper in the dark. The darkness made every step even more treacherous, as I had forgotten to take a torch with me. Anyway, I battled on, desperate not to leave my friend alone in the dark waiting on the other side. I fought through the thick scrub with only the dull light of the moon to help me see where I was going and felt my way down to the edge of the water. I'm not sure what time it was but it must have been in the very early hours of the morning. I was sitting at the bank of the Arm, staring out over the ripples of the water, waiting for my friend. The only sound I heard was the water lapping at the edge of where I sat, and then I heard something moving about in the bush. At first I thought it might have been a wallaby, as I had spotted a few here before. The more I listened the more I realised it wasn't a wallaby. It sounded more like feet pacing back and forth. The sound was coming from under the trees, which I couldn't see through in the dark. There was only one way down to the edge of the cove and it was the well-worn wallaby track, which I had followed— and now there was someone or something pacing where I would need to go to return.

I instantly became very afraid. I had been sitting in the dark for hours waiting for my friend to swim across to me and there was no sight or sound of her in the water; the time she had given me had come and gone hours ago. So I had to deal with the fact that this time she wasn't coming. I also knew that it would be light soon and my mum would discover I was missing and I would be in so much trouble. I knew I had to get back home, but the sound of feet shuffling through the leaves on the ground under the trees continued—it never stopped! I was even brave enough to yell, "GO AWAY!" and still it shuffled. It did pause occasionally but it didn't stop. Eventually, after another hour or so contemplating what I should do, I decided that my mum's wrath would probably be worse than whatever was moving about under those trees, so I bit the bullet and slowly walked towards the sound. I didn't see anything at first as my eyes took time to adjust to how dark it was under the canopy. As I turned left to find the track in the darkness, there standing before me was a small figure, smoke-like and transparent, but definitely a figure, and it was directly in front of me; I had almost stepped right through it! I was frozen in fear in what seemed like minutes but in reality was probably only a few seconds. I had just enough time to take in that the smoky figure was a little smaller than I before I dashed to the right to get away from it.

Once I was at the top of the hill I had time to reflect on what had just happened. Because it was so dark that night I couldn't see where the track was, and the spirit was standing in front of what I thought was the way home. But upon reflection, I realise she was standing in my way stopping me from going the wrong way. If she hadn't been there I would have continued in the dark on a track that led nowhere. I would have most likely slipped and fallen and hurt myself and no one would have known where to look for me as no one knew where I was. I am forever grateful to whoever she was, for making sure I made it home safely that night. I have often wondered why she was there and where she came from. But I'm always glad that she was, even if my heart almost burst out of my chest on meeting her.

My friend never crossed the Arm that night. She told me she had slept in. I don't believe it. I think it was her way of getting back at me for not believing her about seeing a ghost of a young girl in the same area when we were playing there one day. She got me back alright and she sure proved me wrong for not believing her. Even after everything that happened I still swam across the North Arm, but only during the day time!

Desperately wanting to see my friend again, I made my way down to the edge of the water once more. Into the water I went, the reeds tangling around my legs. I didn't care, I felt protected by the unseen. I kept swimming against the current, and was almost half way across when I started to feel tired. For some reason the current felt much stronger that day and I had no choice but to keep swimming or I would surely drown. I started treading water to give myself a break when I noticed a fin come up out of the water about six feet in front of me. A dolphin! How wonderful! I'd always wanted to swim with a dolphin. But as I kept watching the fin I realised it wasn't moving about in a playful way like a dolphin. Uh oh, maybe it's a shark! Now here I am, twelve years old, not a strong swimmer and in the middle of the North Arm, alone and no one knowing I am even here. What am I going to do? I thought. Maybe this is how it all ends?

A calm sensation washed over me and I heard a voice say, "Keep calm, don't splash about or look like you are struggling; just tread water for a little while."

Okay, I thought, as I watched the fin dip back under the water. Woo hoo! It's gone! But then I thought, Oh no, now I don't know where it is, and the water is so dark I won't even know if it's under me or not!

"Keep calm," the voice urged again, so I continued

to tread water but my heart was thudding so hard in my chest I was sure that it would give me away and the shark would come and gobble me up.

"Keep calm," the voice reassured. I was getting very tired after treading water for so long and I knew I had to keep swimming if I was ever going to make it to the other side. So I very slowly and carefully started swimming again. I was terrified but I had to keep going. I cautiously made my way to the other side. It took me at least thirty minutes to swim because I was going so slow and praying the whole way. Once I was safely on shore I vowed I would never ever swim across the North Arm again. And I never did.

I've been lucky like this countless times in my life and have always realised after each experience just how lucky I have been. I have also felt that I must be here for a reason. Why didn't the shark chomp me in two? How did I survive the fall off the ladder? I believe it was more than luck that got me through these situations. I'm sure the prayers of our friends and family helped also. My mother told me I was protected by a guardian angel, and when I was alone I often felt that there was a presence watching over me.

***

At fifteen years and nine months I threw in the towel at school, much to Mum's disgust. You have to go to school, but the bullying and social structures of school all proved too much for me and there was nothing either of my parents could say or do to get me to go back. I'd been slapped, spat on and had bottles thrown at me by a group of girls that made school even more nightmarish than it already was. I tried to explain to Mum how bad it was and eventually she let me stay home as long as I looked for work, which suited me.

I was sitting at the kitchen table with my parents about to eat lunch when a police officer knocked on the door. My mum immediately put her sandwich down and seemed like she knew why he was there. My mind started racing. Did I do something to bring him here? I know I wasn't going to school but the police? I couldn't think of anything I'd done that warranted the policeman, who was still knocking on our glass sliding front door.

My father answered it after a few moments and I can't recall what came next but all I heard was, "Mr and Mrs Patrick, do you have a son named Lance Edward Patrick?"

They answered yes and then the words *he has been murdered* came out of his mouth. Murdered, what a crock of shit! I thought to myself. Who would want to hurt my brother? I couldn't think why anyone would want my brother dead. It must be a cruel joke, I thought.

I was about to get up and punch the officer in the face for making my parents so distraught when I caught a glance at my mother's face. It told me all I needed to know, that it wasn't a cruel joke, it was real, so I steadied myself for what came next. Dad was obviously in shock and he continued to talk to the officer as if what he had just said didn't happen. I guess I was in complete shock also as I couldn't leave my mother's side. I just kept looking at her and at the officer.

So much happened in the next few weeks but most of it is a blur of funeral arrangements and my family's grief. I couldn't understand who would or could do something like that. Someone mentioned taking revenge and to a then-fifteen-year-old that sounded awesome, a life for a life. As I pretended to be asleep, my mother cried herself to sleep every night. I felt totally useless to her. I couldn't change what had happened and I couldn't help her with the financial side of the funeral; I had no clue how to support her. The torment made me want to die inside myself. I think maybe a piece did.

My brother hadn't done anything wrong or sinister. He had knocked off work and headed to the pub for a couple of beers and struck up a conversation with a couple and shouted them some beers. Because of this the couple thought that my brother must have some money and rolled him. They took his life and twenty dollars, a leather jacket, a belt buckle and his boots. I couldn't believe that that's all my brother's life was worth to this couple.

It broke my heart and my faith in the goodness of people. I stopped trusting people and letting them close to me. I felt I was at times too trusting like my brother and I could end up the same way. It made socialising even harder for me and the only time I let people in was when I was drinking.

It took a year before my brother's murder trial began, by then I was working at the chicken shop in Bairnsdale, thirty kilometres away from home, and would walk to catch the bus every day. It gave me some peace to not be a financial burden on my family and at least I could pay Mum board. Both my mother and father went to the trial while I stayed home and looked after all the animals we had. The trial was meant to go for two weeks but lasted three months, due to many problems. I spent my sixteenth birthday going to work and later that night had a small party with my brother and his family. I will forever be grateful that he did that for me. I really needed it.

The trial finished and the couple was found guilty and sentenced to fifteen years. Mum and Dad finally came home, and Mum had a petition for victim impact statements. She busied herself telling people what had happened to her son and trying to get people to sign the petition to get victim impact statements implemented in Victoria. It was while my mum was doing this that I realised her inner strength. She forgave the couple for what they did and I couldn't have been prouder that she let the hate go. She was happier after that, not the same, not back to how she was before, but she stopped crying herself to sleep every night.

When I turned sixteen I had saved enough money from working to buy my first car. I didn't just want any car; I wanted a car with grunt and speed. I fancied the Holden '76 Torana and when I was out driving one day I spotted the car of my dreams. I guess my brother's love of cars had rubbed off on me. It was white and black, a hatchback with an SS in the grill and it was my favourite of all Toranas, a 1976 LX SS Hatchback. I fell in love with it as soon as I saw it. Within a week I had cleaned out my bank account and borrowed enough money from Mum to make it mine. I was so proud to have such an awesome, grumbling sounding beast. I worked hard and nearly every dollar I had I spent on my new passion, getting the Torana ready to be roadworthy, with help from my big bro of course. By the time I turned 18 and got my licence the car was ready and I felt invincible in it. I loved the attention I got driving it, with a 253 engine you could hear me coming from quite a distance. People would turn their heads and stare when I drove past. Strangers would come up to me to talk about the car, and I finally felt like people noticed I was alive! I was alive, young and carefree without a fear in the world, I couldn't care if I lived or not. My parents would be the only people to miss me anyway. So I drove that car fast, as fast as it would go when I found a stretch of road I thought no one was on. Being a small town people had seen me driving like a lunatic and word got back to my family who begged me to slow down. Their pleas didn't go unheard and I constantly had dreams where I would crash head first into a tree and die. I didn't like the dreams, as they always felt so real and made me feel uneasy.

One dark, rainy night I was driving faster than I should have been around a corner and the car started to slide out of control. The loose gravel caused the tyres to lose traction and I quickly found myself sliding to the right. Seeing trees in that direction I wrenched the steering wheel in the opposite direction, and the car began to slide out of control to the left. The trees were thickening and I started to worry that I might not make it out of this. Left, right; I continued to struggle to regain control and straighten the car. It went on and on and felt like five or ten minutes. The whole time I was praying to God to save me and not let me die. What was worse was I had someone in the passenger seat, and if it was to end badly I would make sure the car careened into the trees on my side first. Just when the car began to straighten out, the limited slip diff cut in and spun me around backwards.

I heard a voice in my head say, "If you ever put yourself in a position like this again we will not help you!" I promised I wouldn't as the car took out a speed sign that hit my door, smashing the outside mirror and shattering the glass in the window. My door hit me hard in the leg and I felt a sharp rush of pain near my right foot. I was completely backwards by this time and had no control over the car or what it would hit. I was nearing the state forest where trees were everywhere and I didn't think I had a chance. I was grateful that the trees were on my side of the car though and I braced myself for impact. The car slammed into something so hard I thought I would die from the impact itself. The jolt that brought the speeding car to a halt was indescribable. It took me a couple of seconds to realise I was still alive and a couple more to work out if I was injured or not. When I reluctantly looked over to see if my passenger was okay he was leaping out of the car in a panic. I called to him to see if he was okay but he didn't come back.

The car was slanted my side down, almost as if I had fallen side-on into a large hole. I brushed the shattered glass off myself and tried to open the driver's side door. It wouldn't budge. I quickly decided I needed to get out of the car but I couldn't get out through the window, as it was shattered and jagged. I hauled myself into the passenger's seat which was unscathed. I had to pull myself up into it because of the slant the car was on. I tried to open the door, but I was trembling and the big door was heavier on such an angle. I gathered all my strength and pushed open the door and stumbled to the ground. I stood back for a moment to look at the scene before me and to see what I had hit. Hidden in the long grass was an old tree stump which one side of my car was now sitting on. It was almost a metre off the ground. The tow bar and the petrol tank had taken the hardest impact and were crumpled up under the car. My passenger came out of nowhere and was okay, thank goodness. He decided to go home and get a chainsaw and jack to get the car off the stump. I was so grateful to be alive.

There were a couple of passers-by that night and one stopped and asked if everyone was alright. I said yes.

She said, "I almost didn't stop. I didn't know what I'd find, I thought people would be thrown..." her voice trailed off.

We cut the car off the stump with a chainsaw and I followed in another car and watched my precious car driving sideways down the road. I was so shaken I never wanted to be in a car ever again. Following behind the wreck made me realise how lucky I had just been. I rang my parents as soon as I got home and told them I had been in an accident and that I was okay but I had written off the car. I drank half a bottle of bourbon that night just to settle my nerves so that I could sleep. I kept waking up through the night with the road sign rushing towards me, hitting my door and smashing the glass, Bang! and I would sit upright in bed.

The next morning my brother came over to inspect the damage I had done.

"Can you fix it?" I whimpered.

"I don't think so, Mel, you've bent the chassis. I'm good but not that good!"

I thought my brother was toying with me, which he quite often did. He had to say it a few more times before I realised that he wasn't kidding. He walked over and looked at the roof directly above where I had been sitting. There was a large gash in through the roof like someone had taken a dagger and ripped a tear in it.

"That doesn't look good, Mel." He looked inside and marvelled that whatever it was hadn't ripped the roof lining above my head. "What did that?"

"That's where the sign hit."

"That hit right where your head was. If it went in any further you wouldn't be here."

The image of my nightmare haunted me even more. It took months before I could sleep through the night without the road sign coming straight for me. I was lucky alright, I was lucky I didn't kill my passenger or myself. I wouldn't be able to live knowing I killed someone.

I sold the car piece by piece and decided I wouldn't risk my life or anyone else's like that ever again. I wondered if I was a cat who had nine lives. I was sure that after the car crash I had used all my lives up, and I never forgot what I heard the night of the accident. *They were not coming to my rescue if I screwed up like that again*. It was true, it was my fault; it was all preventable. I kick myself sometimes for losing such a wonderful, rare car, but I'm grateful for the lesson it taught me, that people are more valuable than a car.

Without the lure of the V8 to get people's attention, I slowly slipped back to being on my own, unnoticed by the outside world. I was happy; I started a family of my own and had my first child. She was a real blessing, she came at the right time and I would do anything for her. I wanted the best for my baby girl so I decided to move to Melbourne and go to university so I could provide a good life for my little girl. No matter how much I missed my parents or how tough the assignments were, I was determined to get my degree. With the help of my husband I did.

University was amazing, being a part of a group of like-minded people felt good. I struggled forming relationships with my peers but there were a couple who put me under their wing. I hadn't finished year ten, so for the first year I really struggled. Without their help I don't think I would have survived. I became pregnant with twins while I was finishing my youth work degree. It was a relief to be finished all my assignments when I was struggling to waddle around campus. The stairs were a killer.

I had been working in Out of School Hours Care as I believed that early intervention was crucial in the life of a young person but I was forced to quit working when my father suddenly passed away. I had spoken to him only a few days before and he was unwell with shingles—but no one expected him to become seriously ill from it. The night before my father's passing, I had a dream that I went for my ultrasound and they told me I was having twins. It confirmed what I already knew: I was getting big fast, faster than my first pregnancy so it had to be twins. The next morning I received a call from my sister to tell me that my dad had passed away. I was hysterical. I hoped it was a cruel joke. I grown up with my dad always at home with me, as he had retired when I was quite young. He was my strength, my hero. Before embarking on the four-and-a-half hour drive to Lakes Entrance I decided I should go to my ultrasound appointment that was booked that same morning to make sure my baby was okay. I was still crying while I waited for the scan and they asked me if I would like to reschedule. No, I wanted to make sure everything was okay with my baby before I left.

The scan unfolded just as it had in my dream. I was lying back looking at the screen where I was sure there were two sacks and two babies but I wasn't completely sure. I didn't say anything to my partner sitting beside me. I thought it would be best to come from the physician instead. The physician walked back into the room and broke the news to my unsuspecting partner. The look of shock on his face was understandable after the morning we had already had. I was secretly very happy with myself. I was a little concerned at first until I was told that they were non-identical twins with their own sacks and placentas. This lessened the chance of complications but didn't rule them all out. They wouldn't be conjoined either, which was a huge relief on my mind, as I had seen conjoined twins recently on the television and was concerned by their plight.

Finding out you are having twins on the same day your father passes is a mixed bag of emotions. One minute I was over the moon and so happy that I had not one baby but two growing inside me, and then down I would go with the tragic news of my father's passing. When I finally reached my childhood home I didn't know what to feel. Was I sad or happy? I was worried that if I grieved too heavily for my father I might lose my babies, so I spent the day telling grieving family and friends that I had some good news and that I was having twins. I'm sure they thought that I was being insensitive, but it was all I could do to stop myself imploding. I hoped that the news of twins would bring something to look forward to for my mum.

The rest of the day went by in much of a blur. It was strange though. I felt my dad's energy around and it was like he had gone for a nap or just stepped out to tinker in the garage. At the funeral there was an open casket beforehand for family. I was so scared as I had never seen someone who had passed away before. Mum had always told me that the dead cannot hurt you; it's the living you need to concern yourself with, so I took a deep breath and made my way to my dad. He looked so peaceful as he lay there in his favourite light blue suit. He looked like he was sleeping. My dad was such a prankster and I half expected him to sit up and say BOO! I couldn't shake the feeling that he was still there. I jumped back from the casket just in case the sneaky bugger did just that.

Time passed and I gave my daughter a brother and a sister to play with. The birth of the twins was difficult, as they came seven weeks early and were not breathing when they were born and I almost passed away from massive blood loss. After three weeks in three different hospitals my twins came home with me. I had been home without them for weeks and I hadn't really bonded with them so I wasn't sure I was able to look after two premmie babies better than the hospital could. I asked if I could take them home one at a time but, no, that wasn't about to happen. Later that night as I was drifting off to sleep I felt someone lightly tap my shoulder. My body grew stiff as I knew everyone else was in bed asleep. I opened my eyes and no one was there. My dad used to tap me on the shoulder to wake me up when I was a kid. I was scared so I said, "Please, Dad, don't do that again, it frightens me." It didn't happen again.

Once my babies were home I loved them with all my might but it was a struggle taking care of them both. I survived on next to no sleep. Days, then weeks, then months passed by in a blurred routine of taking care of them and getting my five-year-old to school on time. There were times I thought I wasn't going to make it. I would keep in touch with my mum as often as I could and I struggled to cope with the twins and the desperate need to be with my mum when she needed me the most.

When the babies were older and their sleeping and feeding routines were easier to cope with I would travel with all three kids from Melbourne to Lakes Entrance to see how Mum was. She hadn't been well for a while and was diagnosed with two aneurysms in her chest that caused her much discomfort and pain. She needed me and I needed her. I wanted to move back and help her but I knew the added stress of moving would be too much for me. The older the kids got, the more time I spent with my mum until I spent almost every holiday with her.

Life was easier when my mum was around, life made sense. She understood me and knew who I was on the inside; the likes of which I probably haven't shared with anyone else but my kids and my husband. When I was with her I felt peace, my troubles would slip away and my mum became my world. I could cope with my dad's passing only because I still had her.

When the twins turned three and my eldest was eleven, I decided I would spend my thirtieth birthday with my mum. I hadn't shared a birthday with her since I was a teenager. For June it was a beautiful day. It was cold but the sun was shining enough to warm you. I received some presents and we had some lunch together at home. Nothing special, just being together was special. After lunch I noticed my mum panting badly, she was obviously in a lot of pain. I asked her if there was anything I could do

"No, I'm alright," was her favourite phrase.

I decided that my beautiful little monsters may be causing her some stress, as they were at the age where they were getting into everything, so I decided to take them all to the park in town so she could get some rest. I marvelled at what a gorgeous day it was. The kids were happily running around the playground, the sun was shining and bouncing off the water like crystals. I was with the man I loved and my kids were together and happily playing. I couldn't have wished for a better day. My heart was filled with love and gratitude as we made our way back up the hill to Mum's house. She was looking much better after a rest and I was relieved. We had dinner and afterwards I gave my rambunctious twins a bath. Trying to get them dressed afterwards proved almost impossible as they were darting off everywhere to look at everything in the bedroom, which was my old room. It was like trying to dress two whirlwinds, with me not wanting to tell them off and ruin a perfect day. I decided I would just draw the curtains to gain their attention. As I started to pull the curtain closed, I noticed someone standing outside, a man, just behind the hedge that encased the front yard. I couldn't quite see his face and I was scared if I moved to get a better look he would disappear. It was my dad. I was so happy to see him on my birthday. He was wearing the white T-shirt he always used to wear with a brown jumper over the top. I was happy to see him again and my heart beat a little faster. I was filled with mixed emotions. Is this real? While taking the sight of him in, I got the sense that he was waiting for my mother. He would be staying around until it was her time to go and he would be there to greet her.

I finished dressing the kids and they went into the lounge room to play. I stayed in my old room trying to work out what had just happened and wondered if it were real or if I was going crazy. I realised that when I saw my father I wasn't scared like I had been before; love seemed to radiate from him to me. I had brought Alison DuBois' book with me and started reading it where I had left off. I was at point in the book where her father had passed and it calmed me to read about someone who was going through something similar. I didn't feel so crazy, so I decided that I would go out and tell my mum what had just happened. I decided I would leave out the part that he was waiting for her as I'm sure it wouldn't be of comfort to her. I found Mum sitting at the kitchen table. I took the seat my dad used to sit at, and I struggled to say anything at first. What if she thinks I'm crazy? What if I make her upset? These thoughts whirled in my mind until I finally spoke.

"Mum I'd like to tell you something."

"Yes?" Her eyes always looked at me with pure love.

"I saw Dad."

"When?"

"Just now."

"Where?"

I told her what I had seen outside in the garden. "You're not upset are you?" I asked.

"No, Melanie, I asked him to be here for your thirtieth birthday."

I was shocked. "I wish you had let me know so I could have prepared!".

We laughed about it and moved on. I enjoyed the rest of my stay and returned home to Melbourne. I was on a high after seeing my father again; I had missed him so much, but I couldn't shake what he had communicated silently to me, that he was waiting for my mum.

Then a series of coincidences occurred. One was finding myself having lunch with a complete stranger and from the conversation we had I knew that my mother would pass on a significant day. I sensed that the conversation meant something completely different for him than it did for me. I stayed awake that night trying to work out what I could do to prevent anything happening to my mum. My brain had never let me down yet and I was sure there was something I could do. If not, I could tell someone and maybe they could help me?

I started to struggle with day-to day life with a young family. Sleep hadn't come for a couple of days and I was starting to grow weary. I couldn't let anything happen to my mum; I'd already lost a brother and my dad. My mum was my world and I couldn't lose her. What would you do if you knew someone you loved deeply was going to pass? Wouldn't you do anything to prevent it, if you could? Maybe someone could find a really good doctor to help her? But after five nights without any sleep, my words were not making much sense anymore. On the inside I knew what I was trying to do but to communicate it seemed almost impossible. *Yes, everyone will pass eventually, Melanie, there's no need to get so upset about it.* I knew what they said was right but this was my mother we were talking about and I became even more desperate. The more desperate I became, the less I slept and by the eighth or ninth day without sleep I was having trouble functioning at all. I could no longer look after myself let alone my children; I was on my way to having a complete breakdown, which I did.

I ended up in the psychiatric ward of a hospital. It's funny that I ended up there as I had always wondered what kind of people you would find in there. I always imagined people that were totally insane and murderous, like in the movies. But that is not what I found. They were just everyday people who had lived hard lives that had got the better of them. My heart went out to all of them; they were not the psychopathic maniacs from the movies.

When I recovered from my breakdown, the first thing I did was go and be with my mum. I hated myself for worrying her so much. If only I could tell her what was really happening, she would believe and understand me and help me, as she was the smartest, wisest person I knew. It sucked that I couldn't tell the one person who would know what to do. I was so happy to see her again, so I resolved to let it go and spend every minute I could with her.

My mum's birthday passed and nothing happened, but I still knew she would pass on a significant day so I was concerned about Christmas. I spent Christmas day with my husband's family and then went up to Lakes to see Mum on Boxing Day. Two more significant days had passed without incident so I decided maybe everyone was right, maybe I was being silly and over the top. Mum hadn't been well and she was a lot thinner. This time we talked about everything. She loved seeing the kids, after all, having seven herself that was what she knew and loved.

My mum passed away New Years Day 2007, and there was nothing I could have done to stop or prevent it. I assumed that knowing when someone would pass would give you the chance to change it or do something about it. I felt awful. Knowing and not being able to do anything about it is the worst feeling in the world. Losing Mum made me feel like I had lost everything. I still had my husband and kids but I felt I had let her down and my stupid brain didn't do anything to help me either. The sun no longer shone as brightly as it once had and the birds' songs were no longer as sweet.

***

Now if any of you out there know someone with Asperger's Syndrome, you would know that there is a good reason behind everything that they do. This is the same for me also. I've shared these deeply personal insights into my life so you can see what I mean by the term Indigo: the Knowing, the extra senses used in life to perceive the unperceivable.

Now I knew I was different in the Indigo sense and I thought that was why people didn't like me. My interest in things came from a deeper level. I couldn't play 'hair and make-up' with the other girls when I was concerned about how sad it was that the elderly with all their wisdom and knowledge usually took it with them and only shared some of it with their family. That was one of my first thoughts when I was talking with an elderly lady at age five. So I didn't fit in, so what! I'm glad I didn't. I hope the following poem that I wrote will explain my dilemma.

Always on the Outside Looking in

With knowledge comes power, and I am no longer willing to play the victim in my life. I am going to strive to take my power back I had as a small child before it was taken from me.

Always on the outside looking in, feeling like a stranger within.

Chaos all around me, depression sinking in.

Where have all the people like me gone?

Born an era too late, competition, and materialism is now my fate.

What happened to compassion? Where do I fit in?

Born too late into a world of hate, pettiness is in.

Feeling like a stranger within.

Why is everyone so critical?
Don't they know it damages the soul?

It's filtering down to the children.
What will become of them?

How can they live in a world full of hate?
Quick, rush, don't be late.

You might miss the new big thing!
Blink and it's gone.

What happened to love thy neighbour?

Buy this, wear that, struggling to fit in.

In a rush but headed nowhere, the soul crying within.

True love can only be found with the animals, which are not tainted by the human condition.

Feeling like an alien, why can't anyone see me?

Why can't they see me beneath the skin?

In a rush, buy too much, trying to fill the hole within.

The emptiness inside only growing bigger.

Unconditional love is the only way to satisfy the monster within.

Am I the only one who knows this?

An alien in my own skin, just trying to fit in.

Losing pieces of myself every time I give in.

Becoming fragile now, have to make it in this world somehow.

Always on the outside looking in.

Living in sin as I try desperately to fit in.

Lust, Greed, Envy, Pride, Wrath, become the norm.

Losing pieces of myself, feeling paper thin.

Why can't anyone see the person beneath the skin?

Life is rough, trying to be tough, holding it all in.

I don't know how much longer I can take it.
Just want to give in.

Can't run or hide, hurting deep inside.
Where do I fit in?

Peace, Love, Happiness is what I search for but the
darkness keeps closing in.

Always on the outside looking in.

Maybe there is somewhere, there is a place I belong?

Where people are all banded with a song?

Animals live on instinct, they see the soul within,
maybe I could shape shift?

In their world I would fit in.

Always on the outside looking in.

People all around me, too scared to let them in.

They may crush the soul inside, from them I
must hide.

Fragile and delicate, must protect the child within.

Always on the outside looking in.

Children are much safer, easier to let in.

Sadly watching as the clouds come slowly rolling in.

Hope that they can be strong enough not to let the darkness in.

Always on the outside looking in.

Never alone, but always lonely, searching for people who have kept their light within.

Where are they? The searching has no end.

Sometimes I feel it in the air or on a puff of wind, and I try to keep it in.

Always on the outside looking in.

Times comes speeding in, faster each day, each month, and each year.

The pain is getting stronger now; I don't know how much longer I can keep afloat.

Treading water, the water lapping at my chin.

Always on the outside looking in.

***

This is one of my late-night rambling poems. I find I do my best writing late at night or in the early hours of the morning. I wrote this a year or two ago. I have always been at war with myself, always wanting to fit, yet grateful that I don't. I love my individuality, I cannot be pushed into doing things I do not like to do. Having Asperger's while being Indigo is a dilemma in itself also. The Asperger part of me always needs to know the how, what and why of everything. I have lost many nights' sleep over the previous experiences I've shared with you, trying to work out why it happened. Why am I different? Why do I feel like I do? Why don't I fit in? When I'm feeling good I love my uniqueness; when feeling bad about myself I can wallow in a haze of self pity for months.

At the inner core of who I am, I have always wanted to help others, even though I have so much trouble helping myself. That's why I studied youth work. I would love to help kids who are struggling in many of the same ways as I did. School was a nightmare for me, and apart from a couple of friends, I was glad to leave it behind.

My Diagnosis

I believe that depression is my
emotions' way of letting me know
I have strayed way off my path.

I had been seeing a psychiatrist for a few months for my depression and the fog had lifted a little with the help of medication. I don't like taking medication, I believe it is something that should only be used as a last resort and for the sake of my family, and it was definitely last resort time.

As the fog slowly lifted from my mind, I returned to work as a housekeeper. I liked being a housekeeper; my bosses were nice people who had picked a great group of people to start their new venture with. Housekeeping is hard work, it is physically demanding, and the first couple of weeks left me with pains in muscles I didn't even know I had. I was excited to be a part of something from the beginning. The apartments opened and we put all our training to the test and became housekeepers. Good, honest hard work was how I saw it, and it made me tired enough to fall asleep at night. I needed this job. It was time to move out of my headspace for a while and get back into my body.

I often find it hard drifting off to the land of nod. My husband's head touches the pillow and within minutes his breathing slows to a soft purr. How often I have laid there listening to the light purrs of his dreamtime. At first I was envious of how easily he would fall asleep; I on the other hand can't fall asleep until I have gone through all the things that have happened during the day. Anything that had upset me, startled me or I couldn't quite work out what they meant at the time, would come back at night time for me to replay in my head until I had made some kind of sense of it. I find it extremely difficult to sleep with an unresolved issue still hanging around. Once I have a possible solution I can peacefully fall asleep. I guess it is amazing how my mind can hit record and then at night replay a whole scene of the day with bright colours and all feelings I'd had. It's like watching a movie where you are the main character. I play these movies again and again until I find the solution; it can be very emotionally draining as well as tiring. I've likened it to Post Traumatic Stress Disorder; I can't stop the images from coming into my mind until I have sorted out the problem.

Anyway, with life seeming more balanced, my depression lifted and working gave me the confidence to feel good about myself again. In this state of mind I reflected over my life and could see similarities between myself and my son who is on the autism spectrum. This realisation didn't just suddenly hit me, it revealed itself to me slowly over a ten-year period.

When my son was diagnosed at age four, it didn't come to me as a complete surprise. I knew he was different from his sister. Until he was diagnosed I had no idea what autism or Asperger's Syndrome was. I refused to see my son's diagnosis as a 'disability' as so many people keep labelling it. I prefer to see it as him being unique. I still hate the word disabled or disability as it is not a nice or positive label to live with.

So fast-forward a few years and I'm sitting in front of a psychiatrist telling him that I think I may have Asperger's Syndrome and that is why I feel I have trouble making friendships.

"Okay," he said. "There is only one way to find out for sure and that is to get tested." And he handed me a referral to a psychologist.

In June 2013, a couple of weeks before my thirty-seventh birthday, I was to attend my first appointment. I was nervous and excited; nervous as I had no idea what to expect as an adult, and excited that I may finally understand why I was different. I wanted to know yet I didn't like the idea of being considered as someone with a disability either. You can only change and improve on what you already know. I worried myself about what would happen if I did have Asperger's. How would I tell people? You never know how someone is going to react when you say the 'A' word. (I've heard and seen it wash across their faces when I have had to explain it for my son.) So with the Navman programmed, I ventured out into the night, alone across the city to my after-hours appointment. I really dislike the city at the best of times but driving through it in peak-hour traffic in the dark is hideous! With butterflies swirling in my stomach I battled on trying to find a red house and because it was so dark I drove past it at first. I found a parking space down a side street and looked at the clock. I had arrived an hour early. It was freezing outside and I suddenly—no, desperately—needed to go to the toilet. After almost wetting myself in the car, I gathered all my strength and started to walk towards the red house. I entered at the rear, and the first thing I did was take a quick glimpse around to locate the toilet and ran into it. The toilet was so close to the waiting room, that I'm sure everyone in there heard every little noise I made, which made me feel even more exposed. Feeling super self-conscious and super nervous, I made the quick dash back to the safety of my car. I waited there until my appointment time.

When the time came I returned to the red house for the second time. The waiting room was comfortable and homely looking, with two large sofas on each wall and a coffee table in the middle. On the remaining wall stood a wooden bookshelf and beside that there was a small basket of children's toys. A man and his son exited and I wondered what they would think of my thirty-six-year-old self sitting alone in the waiting room. I didn't have too much of a chance to ponder that thought for long when my psychologist ushered me in to her office. I was offered a chair in the corner of the room. The psychologist introduced herself and started to explain how the session would unfold. I was more interested in her than what she was saying. I wanted to take her in, Can I trust her? I thought. Yes, I think so. She seemed to be a beautiful, understanding person who was professional in her approach. So I started to relax a little and settled back into the chair.

The session began and so did the questions, every area of my life was brought before my eyes, some of it—well most of it—was very painful to re-experience. Time flew and by 8 pm the questioning ceased and the first session was over. The questions had hit upon things that needed to be aired but that had never seen the light of day.

I left her office in a daze, my mind flipping through each and every memory that I had as an awkward teenager, it drove it home to me that it wasn't just likely that I might have autism, I most definitely did. It's one thing thinking you are on the spectrum but it is entirely another knowing you are. I didn't know how I felt about this new realisation. I was happy and sad and angry all at the same time. I was also suffering from reliving experiences that I had long left behind in my past.

With painful memories of taunts and bullying, I found it very hard to fall asleep that night, as the constant barrage of images from the past haunted my sleep. I'm grateful that I had the day off work the following day, as all the memories continued to stir in my mind causing me to relive them again in a different light, in the light of autism. Is that why they did that to me? I thought. I had no idea why people treated me the way they did and I looked at all those painful and humiliating memories with my Asperger goggles on for the first time. It all started to make more sense but with it came more questions. It was extremely painful and saddening to relive all those old memories again and again and it took me a full day to put them back safely in the boxes that had been opened. I had to continually tell myself that these memories were the past and the past cannot hurt me anymore.

During the rest of the week, while I was at work, I tried desperately not to think about autism or being diagnosed. I was to see the psychologist again in a week's time. I would deal with it all again after that session. I threw myself into my life, my kids and my work; and I did broach the subject with my husband. I tried to prepare him for what I felt would soon become fact, that I have autism.

My husband refused to see me as anything but his

wife, mother to his children, and friend. The way he sees me melts my heart and I see him in the same way. It made me love him even more. He refused to see me as having anything 'wrong' with me and I tended to agree with him. I'm just unique, different. I wish everyone I meet could see me the way he does, because I wouldn't need this diagnosis. I've always felt that very few people know the real me, my husband and kids know and my parents knew, but I failed to let anyone else close enough to know. I guess it's a way of protecting my sensitivities from the world.

The second visit to the red house was nowhere near as intense as the first session, though I did rush to the toilet again as soon as I got there. I didn't wait outside in the dark for an hour beforehand this time as I had successfully calculated how long it took me to drive the 28.9 kilometres to get there. I knew who I would be meeting with, what she looked like and also had some idea of what to expect when I entered her office, so I was a lot calmer the second time.

Sitting in the same chair again I was asked more questions about my life and childhood. Questions were fired at me so fast that I answered instantly, sometimes only giving a half answer, as without proper reflection I couldn't give a whole response. It was uncomfortable to say the least. The hour-and-a-half session flew by in no time again, and before

I knew it, it was over and I was driving home through the city. The lights passed by in a blur as I struggled to concentrate on driving myself safely home. My life was flashing before my eyes again, unsettling me and making it hard to drive but I had expected it this time and it didn't throw me off balance as much as it had after my first experience the week before.

With every meeting, I was getting closer and closer to being on the spectrum. How did I feel about that? I really didn't know and with the help of my husband I decided that I wouldn't think about it anymore for now until the diagnosis became official. I had to work the next day and was grateful that we were too busy for me to think about it.

My days were filled with getting the kids ready for school, getting myself to work on time then racing back after work to pick the kids up from school again at three. Then it was working out what everyone would eat for tea and preparing the evening meal. Sometimes I was so exhausted from trying to keep it all together, I would come home and collapse onto the couch and order take-away for tea. Working as a housekeeper left me very tired, as I have explained earlier, but trying to figure out what is going on socially, for me, is even more tiring.

I liked everyone that I worked with but hadn't

formed close friendships with any of them. With the impending diagnosis it made this even more prominent to me. I have been missing out on social cues and communication for over thirty-six years; it was a ground-breaking, heart-breaking realisation for me. How does the world see me? is a question I have often asked over the years but have never found the answer to. I guess my hope is that if given the diagnosis of autism, in the future I can change the way that I communicate with people and hopefully have closer relationships with my peers.

With my thirty-seventh birthday coming up and my children almost ready to break up for the school holidays, I finished work for the day and started to prepare myself for the third and final visit to see my psychologist. With everyone settled and happy at home, I set off in the dark for the final time. I arrived at the red house at the correct time to find my physiologist waiting for me. After a quick pit stop at the now-familiar toilet, I was ready to begin our final session. She had sent me an email earlier in the day letting me know that I could come earlier if I wanted to, but being at work I didn't check my email and apologised for this. That's another thing I seem to do a lot of is apologising, I apologise for everything. This session started differently, and instead of the usual questions I was given a puzzle to complete. It was an easy puzzle but I felt uneasy being observed while completing it. Next I was shown a picture. It was of a group of people sitting at a table in a field and I was asked what I made of it. I felt uncomfortable with the picture and didn't understand why. I took a guess at what I thought it was, and wanted to quickly move on like we had done with the questions. I was asked more questions about the picture but for the life of me I just couldn't describe what was going on. I had a few guesses hoping that that would satisfy her and we could move on, but she just asked more questions about the picture. I answered as best as I could and finally pushed the picture away.

The session continued with more pictures, stories and of course more questions. At the end of the session I was told that I most definitely had Asperger's yet I didn't have the obvious tell tale signs that most people have. What that meant I have no idea. Even though I was expecting this outcome; it still came with a shock and a wallop around the head. My life makes some kind of sense, I guess, in the context of Asperger's, but it raises just as many questions as it answers. Did my parents notice I was different? Does everyone notice how different I am? I was also saddened by the thought that my social blindness may have hurt people or offended them unknowingly and for this I still feel deeply sorry, as this was never my intention. I liken it to an alcoholic who stops drinking and for the first time is able to see the destruction their drinking may have caused their family and friends. I hope that my Asperger traits haven't been harmful to the people who have surrounded me. I also understood why people seemed to sense my vulnerability and used it to their advantage, and this also saddens me deeply.

The thoughts that flew through my mind after being diagnosed came so thick and so fast that I had trouble keeping up with them all. I can only remember a few. Is this how my son felt when I had him assessed? Do my girls have it too?

The diagnosis had answered many questions but it also left me with so many more.

The Report

Nature sings to me and calms me and diminishes all my worries and fears.

I received my report by email and it was both liberating and shocking. Liberating as now I knew why I was the way I was, and shocking because it wasn't entirely correct in encompassing who I felt I was as a person. I think the report shocked me because it casts me in the worst light possible, but at the same time had truth to it as well. In it, it states 'doesn't understand the impact she has on people.' And with my psychologist off on maternity leave I couldn't get an explanation!

This statement still haunts me and has made me question myself and everything that I do even more than I did before. I have never intentionally wished harm on anyone, it's simply not who I am. I have wished for people to go away and leave me alone at times but to hurt them goes against everything I was taught and believe in. I must admit that in my relationships with others I tend to react to negative comments and energies. Mostly I like to run away and hide, especially in situations of conflict that I don't expect. The only people I can have conflicts with are my children and husband, because they love me and I love them and we will always working things out. Despite our differences in understanding we love and care and respect each other enough to resolve the issue. My family are the only people in the world I feel safe enough around to truly be myself. Their acceptance and love drives me to do better for myself and for them. I will continue to do whatever it takes to bring more harmony to all our lives. I believe that understanding and accepting my Asperger's will make me a stronger person, a better wife and mother to my children.

In the process of this I have also discovered that I mustn't lose sight of the fact that I also have many talents. I refuse to see myself as less than anyone else or broken. I have issues I need to deal with, but hey, so does everyone, right? After all, none of us is perfect, we are all works in progress. Understanding my weaknesses and strengthening them won't be an easy task to manage, but nothing worthwhile has ever come easy.

I recently read *Safety Skills for Asperger Women – How to Save a Perfectly Good Female Life*. I'd only read the first chapter and already realised how vulnerable I had been in the past. It kept me up late at night thinking over how easily I'd had the wool pulled over my eyes. It was heart-wrenching. With knowledge comes power, and I am no longer willing to play the victim in my life. I am going to strive to take back the power I had as a small child, before it was taken from me. I'm glad that both my parents passed away before they could see me struggle through this, as I'm sure it would have broken their hearts. I do miss the support and advice they would have given me. My mum, Joy and my dad, Maurice, knew me so well that I never had to explain what I was feeling. They also never misinterpreted what I meant to say, and they always knew I had the best of intentions. They never took things the wrong way like the people in my life do now.

It's very frustrating when people always jump to the worst possible conclusion that has nothing to do with what you are trying to relate. It's frustrating, exhausting, and at times humiliating and lonely. Lonely because life can suck when no one understands where you are really coming from! I miss my parents so much, I think of them every single day. Their understanding gave me a comfort and strength that I am still struggling to find on my own. I know in my heart that my parents wouldn't want me to grieve for them forever; I take solace in the fact that they would want me to live my life to the fullest, being as authentic to who I am as possible. They would want me to do this for myself and my children.

Reflections

How can I leave the world a better
place than when I found it?

The word disability gets used way too much for my liking. Being diagnosed with Asperger's, I cringe when people see it as a disability. Disability suggests that there is something wrong, or of not being able-bodied. When I look in the mirror I see someone who is able-bodied, clever, strong, caring, intuitive and loving. Yes, I make mistakes when I socialise. I might not use the correct words or emotions that are appropriate to the situation, but most of the time it's because I am so super aware of everything and I'm so nervous I'm almost having a complete melt down inside. Most often I'm not trying to be offensive in any way. I'm so busy concentrating and trying so hard to fit in and keep everyone happy that I miss small things like facial twitches and quirks. I don't notice when someone has had enough unless they tell me.

I don't think I will ever understand why neurotypical people always seem to jump to the worst possible conclusion. I have no control over how others take the words I say, I can only hope that they start to feel the emotion behind them.

Up until now, well for most of my life, I've been a victim. It's easy to be taken advantage of when you are not aware of all the rules around you. I'm always so busy trying to fit in that I don't see what's coming until it's too late. Hindsight is not helpful. I do, however, have feelings and senses in my body that tell me that something is not right. When I ignore them, that's when things get really bad. But when I'm near someone and my tummy muscles knot and a bad feeling comes with it, I know not to trust that person. When I listen to what my body tells me I don't end up being hurt. My gut reactions have saved me many times. I still don't think that these things amount to being called disabled though, differently-abled, maybe. But disabled, I don't think so! I wish the word disabled could be swapped with differently-abled or unique, which, in reality, we all are. I like the word unique because it means one-of-a-kind, special, irreplaceable, and every person on the Earth is unique, no matter who they are, how old they are, or what their abilities are. We can look to the animal world to see the harmony of this point of view.

Let's take elephants and zebras for instance. Elephants know they are elephants so they act like elephants and that's okay. Zebras know they are zebras and they act like zebras. Elephants don't want to be like zebras because they already know how important they are as elephants; they are not envious of the zebras either. They both live side by side in harmony with each other because each knows who they are and what they are meant to be. I, like the elephant, know that I am exactly who I am meant to be and I'm never going to try to be a zebra no matter how popular the belief is that zebras are better and we all should be zebras. I will be happy to be an elephant!

I believe we were all born into this life exactly as we were meant to be and our lives have a purpose, which is: how can I leave this world a better place than when I entered it? What brings me peace and helps others? As long as your answers don't affect anyone else in a negative way and you don't have to hurt anyone to get there, then the answers will lead you to what your purpose in life is. Don't ask me what mine is, I'm still working on that. Some are harder than others to work out and just when I think I've got it, I haven't.

I could be wrong, but I believe that people with Asperger's have their life's purpose so strongly etched into their soul, and the urge to fulfil that purpose is so strong that they miss so many little things along the way. I believe that my Asperger's stops me from getting caught up in silly things that have nothing to do with my life's purpose like, Am I wearing this season's clothes? I don't care about the label attached to my clothing as long as it fits and is comfortable. Worrying about these things takes my mind off the big questions in life like trying to find my life's purpose.

The only time I have cared about these things is when I am sad and lonely and desperate to try to fit in. It works for a little while but then I start to feel empty inside even though I have the acceptance of others. It's when I try to fit in to society's norms that I start to feel empty and shallow and that's when the depression clouds start to come rolling in. They remind me to keep going, to push through. I believe that depression is my emotions' way of letting me know I have strayed from my path. I still am not sure what my purpose is, but I know that when I start heading in the wrong direction I feel empty and lost. It's then that I know I need to stop, take a good look around me and work out where I am trying to get to. When I'm headed on the right path, my life is happier, lighter, and I feel brighter within myself. Life becomes easier and coincidences start to occur more frequently. It's a magical feeling that, once gained, you'll never want to be without again.

So now I spend my time meditating and listening to what my instincts and my body are telling me to do. I have always felt my way through life; I cannot trust my eyes alone as sometimes I can be deceived. I thought that everyone felt their way through life but it is only since my diagnosis of Asperger's and long talks with my husband that I have come to learn that this is not so. So I am sharing my experiences with you all, firstly, to give a voice to those who are like me, and also to reach out to others who see the world as I do. I hope that this book paves the way for more discussions on what being on the spectrum means.

My search for trying to understand myself lead me to the library where I could delve into the minds of people who thought much the same as I did. The place I found the most comfort was not in medical journals and psychological definitions—they made me feel worse more than anything. I found true understanding in the pages of the New Age section, where I wasn't schizophrenic if I saw a ghost as a child, or a total nut-ball if I heard an animal speak to me once. I found comfort in many, many books, too many for me to recount here but they have all changed my life for the better.

One of the most significant books I remember is *The Care and Feeding of Indigo Children* by Lee Carrol and Jan Tober. I didn't agree with every single word they wrote but that book completely changed my life. It spoke volumes to me, and it was the first book I ever read that I could totally relate to. And it didn't have the term 'disability' in it once! It describes children who are uniquely special, which all children are anyway, and have great gifts but have trouble with the outside world. These children, being so sensitive, may have allergies to many foods and unnatural environments and additives.

When I was a child and we moved from the city to the country, my health improved dramatically. It was a simple life and sometimes I felt very alone, but I was surrounded by nature, fresh air and fruit trees and the animals around me were my friends. I have never been as healthy as when I lived there, my mind was clearer and less foggy. I was happier and I felt in tune with everything that surrounded me. I was very fit, strong, lean and healthy and it is something that I would like to do for my children, especially my son who is also on the autism spectrum. I think it would do him good to live in the country where I could have fruit trees and my own veg patch. I'll just have to make sure that it isn't too isolated.

My mother and father never knew that I have Asperger's, as they both passed away before my diagnosis, and they never seemed to notice that I was different to other children. If they did know, they never shared their suspicions with me. Sometimes I wonder if my mum intuitively knew that moving me to the country was the best thing she could do for me. Whatever the reasons, she was right, as she so often was. In the country I felt a connection to the land under my feet, the trees blowing in the wind and the animals that called it all home. It is an exhilarating feeling to feel a part of something a little wild and untamed. It was almost as if the land whispered to me of the past, every place holding a memory that I longed to explore. My days were filled with chasing rabbits and trying to catch lizards and grasshoppers. It was bliss for me as nature sings to me and calms me and diminishes all my worries and fears.

I also wonder if Asperger's is God's answer for a world that has become too unbalanced in the race for the material and technological gain. Did he send forth children who only thrive when they are in more natural settings, eating more natural foods? Maybe we are his wish for the world to be more honest and less critical in its approach and analysis of others. I strive to be non-judgemental and more accepting of others, as it is when I feel judged or ridiculed that I feel the need to run and hide and stay away from people. I know I am sensitive, and have often been told that I am too sensitive. But can you really be too sensitive in today's world?

Being diagnosed has answered many questions for me but has raised so many more. For example, if I'm being bullied by someone, is it my fault for not standing up for myself or is it the bully's fault for being so mean? Or are we both at fault? It is my quest in life to find answers for myself and my three beautiful children. If it wasn't for my husband and my children I don't think I would have found the strength to continue to ask these questions, let alone try to find answers to them.

I know that I need more people in my life to help me find the answers to my big questions and many others that I have about life, so I will continue to socialise as much as I physically can without overdoing it. Some days socialising is a real struggle and other days I find it much less so. It seems to depend on the hearts of the people around me. I often look at my neuro-typical husband and wonder how he sees the world and how differently he sees the world to me. I know he loves me, but some days I feel like I am such a burden to him, so I try to lighten the load where I can.

The Spiritual Side of the Spectrum

My gifts of gut feelings, hunches and intuition have saved my life many times, and have also allowed me to escape dangerous situations which at times I have found myself in.

As an adult on the spectrum I feel that treatment plans that only focus on the physical and psychological are not as inclusive as they should be.

People on the spectrum are awkward in their movement, speech and communication skills, and yes, we definitely need to address these issues. But I have found the gap in regards to treatments aimed at people of all ages on the spectrum to be spiritually lacking. I can only speak for myself and my son as I have no idea how other people on the spectrum feel or what they believe.

So based on my life and my knowledge thus far I feel that many services and providers fall short when it comes to encompassing the spirit and soul of a person on the spectrum. I have had many spiritual experiences that some (not all) psychologists would dismiss, disregard and criticise—and worse still— add the tag of insanity to. When I have openly shared some of my private experiences and they have been met in this manner, it has not helped me in any way! If anything, it has made me feel more vulnerable and scared and I have been less able to accept myself as I am. I believe that in order to become a whole and vibrant person we need to acknowledge that people have spiritual experiences and that it is okay if you don't understand them. People on the spectrum may have had these gifts and experiences since birth and have learnt not to share them with others out of fear of rejection. So it is imperative that professionals who work with individuals on the spectrum tread very gently when these topics arise and not to jump to conclusions.

My gifts of gut feelings, hunches and intuition have saved my life many times, and have also allowed me to escape dangerous situations I have at times found myself in.

I believe it would be unjust to disregard these extra-sensory perceptions as hallucinations and other such nonsense, as it could potentially be harmful to the individual. Just because the neuro-typical world doesn't understand or even accept the existence of these gifts does not mean that we should ignore them all together and pretend they are not there. It is the biggest hurdle that government policies need to address and overcome before any person on the spectrum can be fully understood and accepted by the neuro-typical world.

It's not all bad out there, as there are many trail-blazers fighting to be heard: Tony Attwood, Liane

Holliday Willey, Donna Williams, Temple Grandin, Doreen Virtue, Jan Tober and Lee Carroll, Scott Alexander King, just to name a few. Without these people the understanding we have about the spectrum wouldn't be what it is today. I believe we need to push a little more and encompass a physical, psychological and spiritual approach when understanding people on the spectrum. I think governments could be more inclusive of alternative health practices than they currently are today. Meditation, massage and few other alternative therapies are slowly getting the recognition they deserve. I urge everyone to keep an open mind when choosing therapies and treatments for your loved one on the spectrum. And please trust your instincts.

My hopes and dreams for the future are that with more and more men, women and children being diagnosed, and with greater understanding, governments, agencies and professionals in the fields will encompass a more humanistic approach to their practices and start to work alongside the many professionals already working in the alternative fields.

I have noticed over the years that my life flows more easily when I am in acceptance of my spiritual side, I can handle larger groups of people, my conversations with others improves and my life in general flows at a pace I can physically and socially accept. I think it is my path to help meld the two approaches together so that we can all benefit from them.

Acceptance

Everyone has a purpose.

I find more acceptance and understanding from the natural and animal worlds than I do from the human world. I find the natural and animal kingdom to be a place of refuge when the world becomes too overwhelming for me to cope with. I use it as a place to escape to when life gets too hard for me. I have shared this knowledge with my children as I feel it is beneficial to having a healthy state of mind and it creates peace when chaos begins to take its hold on us.

Animals are already well known for their de-stressing abilities. They need to be included more in places where people on the spectrum regularly visit. Fish or even a cat could be used in waiting rooms. Schools are now including vegetable patches and some schools even have a chicken coup. These are all wonderful places of learning and de-stressing at the same time. Being on the spectrum and being a parent to someone on the spectrum does pose many challenges in trying to advocate for my son's needs, especially when most of the time I struggle to advocate for my own. The up side is that I have a unique understanding to how my son might be feeling and I can construct my own ideas of dealing with them. I am by no means a perfect parent and I have made many mistakes along the way, as all parents do. All I can do is try my best and correct my mistakes when I can. There are no steadfast rules about being parent.

I also have two cats that bring laughter and serenity to our house. I chose rag doll cats, as they are very placid and calm and they flop into your arms when you pick them up. My cat's purr brings me to a state of peace where I can rest and then fall asleep.

Special gifts

Sometimes a complete stranger can
come along and turn my day around;
I hope that some days I am that
stranger for someone else.

I believe everyone has special gifts and children on the spectrum are no different. Sometimes their gifts and talents may be a little less obvious but they are still there just the same.

Sometimes a person's gift can be hidden behind an 'obsession' –which is not a word I like to use. With time, every person learns what their gifts and abilities are but they need to be encouraged to keep their passions, while at the same time not live only in that passion.

There needs to be balance.

Energies

Miracles happen to those
who believe in them.

Now I am not sure if everyone on the spectrum feels this, but energies are very hard to explain as they are felt and not seen. In my life I have felt both positive and negative energies. Positive energies are the easiest for me to deal with, as people with positive energies leave me feeling happy and refreshed.

When I sense negative energy I want to run and hide and escape the horrible feelings happening inside me. Places, people, animals and plants all give off an energy that can be felt by a sensitive person. So from the outside you may see me dash from a room and wonder what on earth is going on. Most of the time it is the energy of the people and even the energy of the conversation that has made me feel uncomfortable enough to leave the room. I excuse myself and go outside to smoke. It's not a good coping strategy but it is a socially acceptable reason to go outside when I feel overwhelmed by energy. I hope that in the future I find a more healthy way of escaping rooms full of negativity.

Love

I'm sure there is a touch of magic
in my Asperger's too.

I'm sure that I read somewhere that people on the spectrum are not capable of love. What a complete load of hog wash! I love everyone and every animal and every blade of grass. I have learnt not to show it as it makes me vulnerable to the shady side of society. I hide it as a form of protection so that I don't get hurt. I also do this because anything that does not come from a place of acceptance and love confuses the shit out of me and overwhelms me.

I need to take my time to make sure the people around me are the right people to share my feelings with. I show my children and my husband how much I love them as I feel safe to do so. I'm not an overly huggy kissy type of person but so what! I still love people very deeply. Naturally I would hug and kiss everyone I met if I didn't get the negative energy feedback that I receive. So if I come across you in the street and I seem disinterested, that is not true. I just need some time to deal with the energies that are coming from you before I can get to know you a little better.

Ups and Downs

It takes an enormous amount of
strength to look at your life and find
lessons in your pain and suffering.

Life can be a struggle. When it's good, it can be absolutely glorious, but when things are not going well I can feel as though maybe I shouldn't be here at all. It has been in the low times that I have learnt the most. I realised just how much I am loved by my family and how much I love them. Sometimes a complete stranger can come along and turn my day around; I hope that some days I am that stranger for someone else.

I Don't Want a Cure!

I wonder if Asperger's is Gods answer for a world that has become too unbalanced in the race for material and technological gain?

I believe that my Asperger's is part and parcel of who I am as a person, my most caring and loving side resides in my Asperger's.

So if I were to 'cure' it, I would lose a piece of myself that I value the most.

I'm sure there is a touch of magic in my Asperger's too.

In a Perfect World

In a perfect world I wouldn't have a 'disability' I would be classed as a unique and valuable person who sees the world in a different way.

In a perfect world, my Asperger traits wouldn't matter. If people were less judgemental of others and more accepting, I wouldn't have to worry as much as I do. If people were not so competitive and understood that it is better to bring out each other's strengths, instead of pointing out all their flaws and weaknesses, I wouldn't hurt as much as I do. If everyone understood that life is a struggle for everyone no matter what their circumstances appear to be, I wouldn't feel guilty. If everyone didn't expect anything in return for their acts of kindness, I could pass it on to someone else, and my life would make more sense than it does right now.

I don't expect anything from anyone but I hope for acceptance that we are all different and that I give what I can when I can. If people didn't get offended because I need time to myself, to pull myself together when times are hard for me, I'm sure I would have more friends.

We are not all the same and for this I am truly grateful, we are all made perfect in every way, different yet unique. It would be a boring and unproductive world if we were made exactly the same, with the same mindset and the same set of skills. The world would cease to function. I look at my three children and in them I see the perfection of difference, as each has unique qualities and I cherish their individual gifts. I love them all equally as their strengths are not valued as better than another by me. In a perfect world everyone would see each other in this way and there would be harmony.

In a perfect world I wouldn't have a 'disability', I would be classed as a unique and valuable person who sees the world in a different way. In a perfect world everyone would understand that as long as someone isn't hurting themselves or anyone else than that it is okay to let them be as they are.

Needs

Life works best when you share
it with someone.

In my observations of the animal and human worlds, I've learnt that we all have basic needs that must be met so we can be balanced people and animals. Animals and people share the same fundamental basic needs, like to be housed, fed and loved.

We also have our own individual needs that need to be acknowledged and respected. I have many needs on top of the fundamental need, such as, I like to touch the soft fur of my cat and I like the way it feels against my skin. I need to occasionally hold its fur up to my face; it gives me such inner peace.

I also understand that in return for letting me have my needs met I must respect what its individual needs are so that it too can be happy, such as the need to go outside and the need to be left alone sometimes.

When I recognise and acknowledge my cat's needs it responds to me in a positive way! My poor dog, however, doesn't always get all her needs met, such as being taken for walks and patted often enough.

She is then out of balance and when I'm around her she is all jumpy and horrible. When I don't respond appropriately to my cats' needs they may growl or hiss and run away.

I believe that people are the same and that my Asperger's stops me from telling others what those needs are unless they are a very close friend or family member. And it also stops me from identifying what the needs are of others outside my tight circle. People are so much more complex than animals, so trying to identify what a group of people's needs are as opposed to a single individual is exasperating for me. I find I have more success when talking with people one-on-one, as it is easier.

Relating to animals is so much easier than relating to people because from them I can work out what their needs are. With people it is much harder as their needs seem to change often and I can't keep up. I find it even harder still to ascertain what it is they need from me. Sometimes I am unable to give them what they need as it is in direct conflict to my life's purpose and what I need to be doing to stay on my own unique path.

I hope that this makes sense, as I am simplifying something that is much more complicated than I can explain or understand myself completely. Though this is how I see my life. I think that's why I can relate to children and the elderly better than

I can with adults, because their needs are much less complicated and are much easier for me to identify and meet. I can also identify when a child is unbalanced by their behaviour, as their behaviour lets you know whether their individual needs are being met or not. When my children are upset and miserable, they need help in making sure I am meeting their needs. (Needs not wants, there is a difference). If only people could see a child and instead of thinking, what a naughty child, thought, this child is a little out of balance, what can I do to help change that? life would be better for all of us I think.

Life is so complicated, messy and hard at times and we can't be everything to everyone all the time, so that's why I think my city of Melbourne would benefit having a service like Green Chimneys in America. Green Chimneys is a farm and a school, which encompasses both elements in educating young people while caring for animals. It is a partnership that I think could be used with people on the higher end of the autism spectrum who fall short of getting into autism schools in Australia. Animals can help start successful relationships with others.

Everything happens
for a reason

It would have been awesome and beneficial to me to have my areas of strength diagnosed.

I have learnt so much from the times in my life when I have been at my lowest. We all have suffered in some way, but the people I look up to the most are people who come through great tragedy or sorrow and come out the other side as better people.

It takes an enormous amount of strength to look at your life and find lessons in your pain and suffering.

I believe we have two choices. We can let our woes and problems overtake us and become bitter and cold and take it out on the world around us, blaming others for our predicament (the result of which takes us nowhere!), or we can learn as much as we can from the situation, see the lessons we have learned from it and apply it to our lives in a positive way, becoming better people as a result.

With every mountain I climb and every trouble and pain I encounter, I learn from it, grow from it, take that part with me and try to leave the rest behind where it belongs. I am not always successful and have found myself in hospital for depression three times. Thank God I grew up around horses as I was taught if you fall off you need to get right back on again. I won't lie, it isn't easy, it's not a life of the faint of heart, but with every hurdle I scrape over I think of my children and I try to pass the lessons on to them.

I Have Learnt

Our education today only prepares
us for a small percentage of the jobs
that will be available in the future.

I've let my life troubles pull me down to the pits of despair so deep I thought I would drown. Life was never meant to be easy, but I think it is a school where we need to learn from everything and everyone around us with no judgement. I've learnt that we are all different and that's okay. We don't all see the world the in same way, and I'm glad. Life would be boring if we did everything the same. I also believe that every person who comes into my life has something to teach me. Sometimes I learn negative things about myself and I learn and try to change them. I've also learnt that life works best when you share it with someone, as we were never meant to be an island unto ourselves, even if the world makes you feel like you want to run and hide inside, shut the door and never go outside again. Take some time to be by yourself and meditate, but never give in to it!

I have learnt that no two people are the same and that I should never judge a book by its cover. I've learnt that forgiveness is the only way forward and when you don't forgive you get stuck and have to re-learn lessons. I have learnt that miracles happen to those who believe in them. That the saying, like attracts like is true, and what you think about the most is what you draw towards yourself. Life is not worth living if I'm thinking of only myself and I need to include others in my thoughts every day.

I have learnt that upon waking in the morning I should be grateful for at least three things. I have also learnt that our children are ours only for a short time, so we teach them the best we can and then we have to let them live their own lives. (This one is going to be hard as I haven't quite got there yet and cannot imagine my life without one of my children living with me). I have learnt that sticking up for myself is not a sin; it is purely for my own protection. I cannot control others at all; I can only offer guidance when it is asked for. We all make mistakes and that's okay, as long as we learn from them. You cannot keep doing what you have always done and expect things to improve or change for the better. You need to change yourself first then everything else follows.

So many people and books have taught me these lessons and I cannot remember exactly where I got what from but the ones that come to my mind first are included in the list of further readings at the end of this book.

Mentorship Program to Coincide with Autism Funding?

Green Chimneys is a farm and a school. It encompasses both elements in education for young people while caring for animals.

I think kids on the spectrum could do well matching their special interest to older people in the surrounding community, who share their interests. My son's first love at the age of three was cows, if I had a mentor in the wider community who worked or lived on a farm and was willing to teach my son, he would have been able to live out his dream and it would no longer be called his obsession!

My own first love was of horses and as a child if I could have been mentored by a stockman I would have fulfilled one of my lifelong dreams also.

Obsession is a terrible word; I would rather change it to passion. People on the spectrum have a specific purpose in life and need to follow their interests. If my parents could have accessed a mentorship program that matched my interests, I would now ride like a stockman, write like a poet and play the piano. Instead of pursuing my passions I desperately tried to fit in to a world that has underestimated the knowledge of the past.

There is still value in learning these things, as everything seems to go in circles. What isn't cool now will come back into fashion in the future.

I hope we listen more to our spectrum friends and let them be themselves and be respected for it. We need them as they are.

Indigo or Asperger's?

It's your strengths that get you through the tougher times.

I identify myself as having Asperger's, as I most definitely do, but the problem I see with this diagnosis is that it only covers my deficits and flaws and focuses on changing me to become more 'mainstream' and I don't believe I ever will be, no matter how hard I try to 'fit in'. I feel I have lost some of my Indigo traits, the things that make me unique and special. Just because I am different to the majority, does this make my views and opinions of the world wrong? It is terrible growing up with only a couple of friends. Are we all only important if we are revered by our peers? Do I need to be loved by many to be seen as important? The culture of the time is that the more you are alike the more popular you are, which I have never really understood as it takes a unique thinker to stand out alone and sometimes to suggest changes that others might not see. I'm writing this now feeling extremely isolated. I know a lot of people yet I have very few close friends who understand me.

Under the heading of Indigo, the views change and my life makes more sense, there are others out there like me who see the world from a different perspective like I do. I walk the Earth feeling a lot like a mirror, I just reflect back what is sent my way. The energy of animals is much more natural and accepting. They don't mind my uniqueness and accept me for who I am. I reflect this to them by accepting them as they are and I think that is why my relationships with the animal world has always been my saving grace during my hard times. People are messy and complicated, they inflict pain on others to make themselves feel better, and this is the thing that I cannot understand, as I believe we are not here to hurt each other but to help each other reach our goals and find our purpose in life. We were never meant to be in competition with each other, we need to be more like puzzle pieces, uniquely shaped and completely perfect as we are. We just need to find where we 'fit'. We need to keep exploring until we find where our place is, where our puzzle piece fits in perfectly with the others around us. We were never meant to be shaped all the same, we were meant to be different, so one day the jigsaw puzzle of life can fit together to make the world a better place for all.

I agree with Lee Carroll and Jan Tober in their book, *The Indigo children 10 years later*. Our children are changing and old systems that are in place now are not relevant anymore, especially our education structures. They have changed some, but nowhere near enough to deal with the amount of children that are now being diagnosed as being on the spectrum. It is these children that the current education system is failing. Our education today only prepares us for a small percentage of the jobs that will be available in the future, as the way in which we live and work is changing so fast that schools cannot keep up. That's why I believe we need more schools like Green Chimneys in America. Education needs to become more focused on what the children need to learn and not what they should be taught. Our children are brighter than they are allowed to show. The rigidity of education systems, I believe, is holding our children back. Schools in Australia have changed a lot since I was at school and they are moving in the right direction but they are unable to successfully help those kids on the spectrum as much as they could because they have such strict guidelines of what needs to be taught. I think too much importance is put on achievement levels and not enough emphasis is put on learning to navigate through life's ups and downs. Learning places like Green Chimneys are successful because they focus on these things.

The trouble with having Asperger's is that there is too much focus on IQ. Having a high IQ doesn't always spell success; people with high IQs need help and understanding also. Being diagnosed with Asperger's syndrome is helpful as it clearly shows where my weaknesses lie and I need to strengthen those areas, but I've always been somewhat aware of them. Once diagnosed it would be beneficial to me to have my areas of strength diagnosed as well as those things I never see for myself. Other than your parents, people don't tend to celebrate your strengths with you but they are always eager and quick to point out your flaws. It's your strengths that help get you through the tougher times and if you don't know what they are and are always judged on or noticed for your flaws then no matter what your IQ is you are destined to fall.

Maybe that's why so many people with Asperger's find themselves in depressive states. I know that's why I have been so down on myself, because I find it extremely hard to see what my strengths are. My dream would be to see something like Green Chimneys open in Australia although it would also include meditation, yoga and alternative health practices. The inclusion of animals in a setting like this could be so beneficial to those on the spectrum. Please check out the Green Chimneys website if you'd like to know more. What they are doing is amazing and I would love to be a part of something similar in Melbourne, Australia.

Thank you.

Further Reading

Liane Holliday Willey, *Pretending to be Normal/ Living with Asperger's Syndrome* and *Safety Skills for Asperger Women – How to save a perfectly good life*

Tony Attwood, Apple Podcast, *Women with Asperger's* Radio Program (and everything he writes and co-authors)

Lee Carroll and Jan Tober, *The Indigo Children* and *The Indigo children 10 Years Later (What's happening with Indigo teenagers)*

Ruth Schmit Neven, *Emotional Milestones*

Doreen Virtue, *The Light Worker's Way* and Angel Card Decks

Louise Hay, *You Can Heal Your Life*

Wayne W. Dyer, *There's a Spiritual Solution to Every Problem*

Paulo Coelho, *The Alchemist*

Hanneke Jennings, *Love Is The Key*, Masterclass Series

Further Reading

Dedication

My heartfelt thanks to Animal Dreaming Publishing, especially Trudy King for all the help in bringing my manuscript to life. Without you I couldn't have done it. Thank you for being so understanding when I didn't have a clue as to what I was supposed to do next!

I would also like to thank all my family and friends for always believing in me and supporting me in my endeavours to become a published Author.

My heartfelt thanks to you all.

Melanie

About the Author

Melanie Ockwell is a wife and mother of three who lives in Melbourne, Australia. Melanie believes that animal-assisted therapy should be available to all those on the spectrum, and would love to be a part of the opening of such a place in Melbourne's northern suburbs.

America has 'Green Chimneys', which successfully combines animals and troubled children, and just think – where would Temple Grandin be without her love of cows?

Australia could benefit greatly by having something similar to 'Green Chimneys' for those on the spectrum.

You can join the group Indigo/Aspie on Facebook if you would like to be involved in getting an animal-assisted therapy centre open in Melbourne's northern suburbs. Join Melanie in making this dream a reality.

Moonchild

I first heard the name 'Moonchild' when, as a little girl, I watched the magical movie, *The Never Ending Story*. Moonchild was the name given to The Childlike Empress by the main character, Bastian, when she – in order to save her life – she must be given a new name by a human child. As a Cancerian, and because I am astrologically ruled by the energies of the moon, I've always felt a strong connection to the moon.

Growing up, I loved nothing more than riding my horse at night, with only the light of the moon to guide us. Moonlit nights were my favourite time to spend with the horses because, in a magical way, everything seemed different, with the moons slivery beams being the only source of light. The way the moon looks when its image is reflected in water, especially the sea, a small pond or lake, makes my heart sing. I've always felt a strong connection to the moon. I love its soft glittering light. And even as a grown woman, I still love the moon and how it influences the tides – and all of humanity as well.

Moonchild

I first heard the name 'Moonchild' when, as a little girl, I watched the magical movie, the Never Ending Story. Moonchild was the name given to The Childlike Empress by the main character, Bastian, when she – in order to save her life – the must be given a new name by a human child, Asa Cancelian, and because I am astrologically ruled by the energies of the moon, I've always felt a strong connection to the moon.

Growing up, I loved nothing more than riding my horse at night, with only the light of the moon to guide us. Moonlit nights were my favourite time to spend with the horses because in a magical way everything seemed different, with the moons silvery beams being the only source of light. The way the moon looks when its image is reflected in water, especially the sea a small pond or lake, makes my heart sing. I've always felt a strong connection to the moon, I love its soft glittering light. And even as a grown woman, I still love the moon and how it influences the tides – and all of humanity, as well.